Dog is God Spelled Backwards:

Lessons I Have Learned From My Dogs About My Heavenly Father (And Other Stories That Have Struck My Fancy)

Michael Ellerbe

CROSSBOOKS

CrossBooks™
A Division of LifeWay
1663 Liberty Drive
Bloomington, IN 47403
www.crossbooks.com
Phone: 1-866-879-0502

©2011 Michael Ellerbe. All rights reserved.

No part of this book may be reproduced, stored in a retrieval system, or transmitted by any means without the written permission of the author.

First published by CrossBooks 03/21/2011

ISBN: 978-1-6150-7739-7 (sc)
ISBN: 978-1-6150-7742-7 (dj)

Library of Congress Control Number: 2011922581

Printed in the United States of America

This book is printed on acid-free paper.

Any people depicted in stock imagery provided by Thinkstock are models, and such images are being used for illustrative purposes only.

Certain stock imagery © Thinkstock.

Because of the dynamic nature of the Internet, any web addresses or links contained in this book may have changed since publication and may no longer be valid. The views expressed in this work are solely those of the author and do not necessarily reflect the views of the publisher, and the publisher hereby disclaims any responsibility for them.

———————— ————————

All proceeds from the sale of this book will go to Refined By Fire Ministries, Inc., a 501(c)(3) tax-exempt corporation.

To learn how you can partner with RBF to help be a part of the solution to mass incarceration across our nation, visit our website at www.rbf.la.

Refined By Fire Ministries, Inc. (RBF) was established in 1989 having been co-founded by Michael, his wife, Elain and their daughter, Ari. The organization was incorporated in 1995 as a non-profit organization with an initial mission to provide religious programming in adult and juvenile corrections facilities. The organization has seen its mission expand to now encompass a focus on re-entry activities to include pre-release and post-release life skills educational programs for offenders approaching release and for their families. RBF's mission is:

To partner with corrections facilities, community- and faith-based organizations to enhance and expand life skill educational programs to assist the incarcerated, the ex-offender, and under-resourced individuals as well as their families, in accessing needed resources to experience success upon release and improve their quality of life.

The vision of the organization is to ensure that the incarcerated as well as segments of the state's under-resourced population who are at-risk of committing crimes leading to incarceration are provided sufficient resources to re-direct their lives through educational life-skills programs as they strive to be restored to their families and become contributing members of their communities. Through RBF's latest initiative, **Reentry Benefiting Families**, the mission and vision of the organization is being carried in partnership with correctional facilities and other faith- and community-based organizations.

──────────── ────────────

ACKNOWLEDGEMENTS

Now before you throw rocks at me and say "how could I compare God with a dog", I'm not. What I am doing is comparing the chasm of intelligence between me and God with that between me and my four-footed children, Biscuit, Catfish, Blueberry and Highway. What about the "And Other Stories That Have Struck My Fancy" part of the book, you ask. Well those are thoughts that I've had and figured that if I wondered about these things then so did others. I may be wrong but I strongly believe that many of you are as warped as me. No really, don't thank me for the compliment, I really mean it.

As with any endeavor others need to be thanked. First, thank you Father for letting me see these things with an eye that maybe sees how some of us--who aren't the sharpest knives in the drawer--see things. Thank you Elain, my bride, for being smarter than me and hounding me, (get it, HOUNDING me. . .I know I'm sad) until I put these stories on paper and for being the cutest and best friend I've ever had. To Ari, our daughter, as ridiculous as it may sound, for being deeper than me. You encourage me by just being you. You don't give up and like your mother, you strive to always be the best you can possibly be always giving God the glory for any accomplishments. To Chet, the most marvelous outstanding son-in-law anyone could ever hope and pray for, thank you for taking care of our little girl and being the support you have been to our family. Many thanks too to Cindy & Jim Patterson for their friendship, support, Cindy's editing expertise and Jim volunteering her!!

And last, but certainly not least, my four furry children, this book definitely would not have been possible without your antics, off the wall personalities and your never ending love no matter what!

Well, sit back and enjoy this short book of short stories. If you think it's funny and helps you understand a few more things than you did before you read it, tell your friends. If you don't like it, keep it to yourself, my psyche is fragile and my feelings are hurt easily. Either way, I pray that maybe these foolish little stories will help you have a better understanding of our relationship with our Heavenly Father who loves us more than we can ever possibly imagine and who wants true fellowship with us his children.

- **Michael**

BISCUIT & CATFISH – BEFORE THERE WAS BLUEBERRY & HIGHWAY

Biscuit, also referred to as King Biscuit, Little Baby Biscuit, Roly Poly, and let us not forget, Little Rotten Biscuit, came into our lives in December, 2000. A month earlier, we had just put our beloved 13 year old Dalmatian, Bueller, (named for Ferris Bueller), down due to an untreatable kidney disease. Our hearts were broken and we swore "no more puppies" for what we thought would be a long time. How could any dog replace Bueller? Well, we thought wrong and God knew what we needed—the perfect puppy—Little Baby Biscuit. If you really don't want to adopt a little ball of fur, don't go to the PetsMart on a Saturday during adoption days, pick one up and expect to actually be able to put him back in the cage. And that's how Biscuit became a part of our family. He now rules and reigns for all his 30 pounds as the Alpha of the pack (including over us most times!!) Just don't let the Dog Whisperer know!!

Catfish, also known as Biscuit's Baby Brother, Big Slurp, the Galoot, Dinosaur Head, Big Baby Catfish, Fishes and The Fish, was welcomed into our household in the Spring of 2002. Again, we say, if you don't want to adopt a puppy, don't let your daughter go to PetsMart on adoption day because you are likely to get a phone call that goes something like this: "Dad, there is the cutest LITTLEST (key word here) puppy that needs to be Biscuit's brother. He is the last one in his litter and he's all by himself. Can I bring him home?" What are you going to say at that point?? So, 60 pounds later, we have the cutest, not so little Catahoula Cur, with the sweetest personality you will find in a 60 pound hound dog as a member of our household.

It was the antics of these two that began my journey in relating my relationship as the "father" of these two four-footed furry children to my relationship with my Heavenly Father as His child. As the Bible tells us in 1 Corinthians 1:27 God will use the foolish and the weak things of the world to make a point. I know me and my pups fall into one or both of those categories. I hope you not only enjoy reading our stories, but come away with a new perspective on how much our Lord loves us and wants the best for us.

ALL HE WANTED TO HEAR WAS MY VOICE

"My sheep hear My voice, and I know them, and they follow Me;"
John 10:27 (New American Standard Bible)

One night some time ago, I let Biscuit out for his evening constitutional and back yard patrol. To his amazement and terror, there was a killer cat which belonged to a neighbor on our back patio. This caused Biscuit grave annoyance and concern. It scared the daylights out of him is what it did. Once I was able to coax him back into the house (which really took some effort). How would you like to have to walk past a lion to get into your house? He was very upset and scared to death for quite some time. I sat with him, stroked, petted, talked to him for quite a while. Now I know one of the things you are possibly saying right now, is "he pays too much attention to that dog, he needs to get a life". There's another thing you could be saying and that is "Michael, Biscuit is a dog, he can't understand what you're saying." Well I'm not here to argue that with you although he most assuredly knows: eat, treat, go, come here and have you lost your mind? Wait, that last one's what Elain tells me, never mind. But for the sake of argument, let's say you are right. The point is this. He really didn't need to totally understand what I was saying. All he really needed was to hear my voice softly encouraging and comforting him. The words weren't as important as the tone in this case.

Isn't that what we need sometimes? Not necessarily the "perfect" words, but just some words of comfort, encouragement in a voice filled with love and care. I have been to many funeral homes where all I could say was, "I'm here and I love you." Very often that's what we want and need to hear, "I love you and I'm here." Great thought isn't it?

I'll tell you Someone who is always there, even closer than a brother. His name is Jesus. He always has been, He always will be. No problem too great. Not problem too small. No person too ugly. No person too beautiful. He loves us all. So much that He paid a debt for us that He didn't have to pay and we couldn't pay. That's love.

If you haven't found Him, do so. Jesus wants you to and He isn't hiding. If you haven't found that church home, keep looking. It's out there.

We're all like Biscuit sometimes. All we want to hear is a quiet voice that lets us know, just by its tone, that everything is going to be alright. With Jesus, it will be.

———————— ————————

.....AND I'LL FORGIVE YOU THEN, TOO.

"...But Thou art a God of forgiveness, gracious and compassionate, slow to anger and abounding in lovingkindness;..."

Nehemiah 9:17

I am not writing this in the best of spirits. Matter of fact, I'm about as mad as a wet hen, however mad they get. Catfish, the demon child addition to our family, has me in this state. For those of you who don't know Catfish, he's why you don't let your daughter go to PetsMart on Saturday's when they have puppy adoption going on. He is The Mighty Biscuit's new brother. We call Biscuit and Catfish, Deuteronomy 28. You know, the Blessing and the Curse. Guess which one Catfish is?

Anyhow, why I am fit to be tied. We are doing our best to train Catfish to be a house dog. Thus far it isn't working. Unless of course, you live in a pigpen, and there are still some things that Catfish does that pigs wouldn't put up with. This is what I arrived home to with Catfish the Horrible having done the following: torn up the mail, fertilized the carpet TWICE, watered same, torn the insulation gasket off of a door, umbrellas were in the living room, the umbrella stand in the kitchen, and I found some root of some plant from "I know not where" which had been mangled all over the kitchen floor. Did I mention the fertilizer?

Death should have come quickly and painfully. But did I? No-o-o-o-o!. I'm way too nice a guy for that. I cleaned it all up, after some nose rubbing, his not mine. Cleaned my shoe which was so kind as to find the fertilizer (did I mention that?) for me. And then explained in a not-too-quiet voice that he shouldn't do these things if he wants to remain a member of this family. Of course, all the time, Biscuit, like any good brother was saying; kill him, kill him, kill him. But again, I didn't. He did however, spend a great deal of time outside after that. The whole time whining and crying about how unfair this was and that he was only doing what comes naturally to an animal.

When he was allowed to come back in to the house we had a talk. First, I told him that I still loved him. Second, I told him that no matter how much I did love him, I would not tolerate this kind of behavior. I cannot let unacceptable behavior go unpunished. If I do, why shouldn't everybody do the same? After all, we're all just animals, according to some, and we just do what comes naturally to animals.

He looked at me with those big brown hurt puppy eyes and basically told me with his actions that he would never, never, never, never, never do that again. My response, "Yes you will." And do you know what will happen if Catfish is repentant when he, shall we say, messes up. I'll punish him again, I'll forgive him, but I'll never stop loving him. Why? He's mine, that's why.

There's Someone who loves you that much also. Even when you "fertilize" your life and the lives of others, He still loves you. Go to Him, take your punishment. He'll forgive you, pick you up, dust off your knees and show you how He wants members of His family to be. Oh, and Catfish, he's still a member of the family. It's just taking a long time for him to grow up and understand what will and will not be allowed in our family. But, when you think about it, doesn't it take all of us a long time too?

BE GOOD WHILE I'M GONE

"Do not let your heart be troubled; believe in God, believe also in Me. In My Father's house are many dwelling places; if it were not so, I would have told you; for I go to prepare a place for you. If I go and prepare a place for you, I will come again and receive you to Myself, that where I am, there you may be also."

John 14:1-3 (New American Standard Bible)

Catfish, be good. These are words we say to the demon puppy when we leave the house to go any place. These words might as well be, "Catfish, while we're gone, why don't you fly to the dark side of the moon and get us a bucket of cream cheese." That's how farfetched it is that he will be good. These are words and phrases that should never be written, spoken or surely never expected together. He'll do whatever he wants to do and we'll deal with it when we get back. When we get back we may find our house, our home, the most expensive investment we'll ever make turned upside down, chewed up, messed up, messed in, and maybe even moved to a different location.

"Catfish, be good." These are actually two phrases that are mutually exclusive of one another. He's not going to be good. He's going to be himself. If he feels good that day, we're in good shape. If not, we come home to surroundings that make rodeos look tame.

Here's the problem, Catfish is just doing what comes naturally. He, at his age, doesn't know exactly what "be good" means. He is only doing "what comes natural", have you heard that excuse? I remember the vet telling us in order to help "house break" him so he wouldn't fertilize the carpet, we needed to take him outside immediately after he: wakes up, eats or finishes playing hard. My first thought, "what else do puppies do?" It's not like he needs to do this after he finished his math homework or shooting pool (and we know that dogs can do that--we've seen the velvet picture). Catfish, the Vicious Fish, hasn't had enough of a history with us to know what we expect of him. He's still the curse of the Ellerbe household, more of a pain than he's worth. Cute is the only thing that keeps him alive. (Not like his perfect brother, Biscuit.)

However, there's hope. The more Catfish hangs out with Biscuit, the more he sees how Biscuit acts and what the rewards are for behaving the way we want him to. Oh sure, we know that he loves us. He can wash our faces with his tongue in about five seconds and his rear end nearly falls off because he wags his tail so hard and fast when he sees us. But he still "messes up," double meaning meant. We still love him and therefore we don't give up on him.

God does the same thing with us. He put us on this planet and told us to be good. We thought good and stupid were interchangeable words and so we acted, and still today, act that way. Did God give up on us? Nope. He sent us His Son to show us how to live with God, each other, and even ourselves.

Know that today, you can't be good on your own. Not good enough anyway. We need to have an example, a mentor, someone to show us how to live and how to be. Fortunately, we do. Again, His name is Jesus. If you will turn to Him today, He'll show you right from wrong, acceptable, from unacceptable, up from down. Also, He'll change your life so that your forever will be at home with God despite all of the "mess ups" we've committed in our lives.

What are you waiting for--an invitation? Ok, here it is. God's inviting you to come, sit on His lap, let Him hold you and show you the way He wants you to be. You may say, "I like doing things my way and my way only." Question, "how's that working for you so far?" It's time to change, don't you think?

———————— ————————

BISCUIT GOES TO WHERE THE BLESSINGS ARE

"I call heaven and earth to witness against you today, that I have set before you life and death, the blessing and the curse. So choose life in order that you may live, you and your descendants."

Deuteronomy 30:19 (New American Standard Bible)

On a scale of 1-10 weird, I suggest you get a higher scale for another way Biscuit has trained me. In the mornings, when I sit on the edge of the bed to put on my socks, Biscuit will come in front of me, and when I cross my legs to put on my socks, he expects me to scratch his back with my foot. Here's the picture, I'm sitting legs crossed, sock in hand, just attempting to do what people do all over the world every day, and I, yes I get to scratch a dog with my un-socked foot.

For a total picture, you need to imagine Catfish lying upside down on my left, getting me to scratch his stomach, Blue and Highway vying for a place on my right, and Biscuit getting scratched by my foot. Do you have a picture in your mind? I don't want that picture in mine. I look like some kind of human whirly-gig going in all directions to satisfy everyone else. Please remember, when I scratch Blue or Highway, I must have enough time, energy, and hand to scratch the other one also. Sometimes it amounts to me leaning my head on Number Four, whoever that is at the time, and baby talking that one in order to appease.

But back to Biscuit and this ritual du jor. I haven't a clue how this got started, but it did. One day I wasn't doing this, the next day I was. Now, to stack weird on top of weird, when I change feet in an attempt to put my other sock on my other foot he moves. He now goes to where the other leg is crossed, that foot is at the right angle and gets his back scratched from that direction. Got the picture again? A while in one direction with one foot, a while in the other direction with the other foot. Biscuit has learned to go to where the blessings are, Dad, morning, bed, socks, scratch.

This is something we need to learn. We need to learn to go to where the blessings are. Have you noticed that human beings have a bad habit of planting garbage and expecting roses to grow? We hang around in the worst places, with the worst people, with the worst attitudes and just don't understand why our lives aren't any better. There's a very old saying, "lay down with dogs, get up with fleas." Why are we surprised when this happens? You're not going to meet Mr. or Ms. Right in a club at 2:00 a.m. If you hang around people with negative attitudes, you'll develop one too.

Go to where the blessings are. One of the most amazing things in my life is the attitude of some people--they tell God to leave them alone and then get mad when He does. Let's work through this slowly. You tell Him to leave you alone, then you get out done with Him when you suffer the consequences of your decision, and the fact that He granted you your request. If this is you, hit yourself on the head now.

Go to where the blessings are. You want good things to happen, hang around with good people. Is this the formula for the perfect life? Of course not. Fleas can sneak onto the best and cleanest puppies there are. Suffering will come into the lives of the finest saints on the planet. But, if we want to have a better chance at a better life, once again, go to where the blessings are.

Help yourself to go--to His people, to the thousands of books that offer ways to view things with a positive eye. Might I suggest one book to start with? How about the Bible? It has some great stories, lessons, a biography that is second to none, and some great answers to life's issues. Go to where the blessings are. The journey isn't that far.

BUSTER KEATON PUPPY

"Clouds and thick darkness surround Him. . ."
Psalm 97:2 (New American Standard Bible)

Those of you who have pets, especially dogs, may have a name for your pet but also may have nicknames based on some of their weirder personality traits. Biscuit has many. One of them is Buster Keaton Puppy. For you who don't know who Buster Keaton was, he was a physical comic during the days of the silent movies. No I'm not that old but I do recognize art when I see it. Buster Keaton was known as the Great Stone Face. Where this came from, if I remember correctly, was that at one time he performed with his father in circuses and vaudeville doing physical comedy. He would be thrown about by his dad, bounce off of things, jump back up and never show any emotion. He kept his face impassive and showed no effects of the rigorous acts that he had just been through.

Biscuit can do the same thing. He will sit there, look at you and have no emotion on his face, in his eyes or even in his ears, just kind of slumped down. Not that he doesn't care, he's just sitting there and I can't read him right then. But please understand this, Biscuit loves me. I know some of you might say, "animals are incapable of the emotion of love". I'm not here to argue that with you. He wags his tail, jumps all over me and doesn't want to leave my side when I get home. Wait a minute, that's how I am with Elain also. Anyhow, because of years together, snuggling, scratching, just being together, I know that he loves me and I love him.

Sometimes we look for and look upon the face of God and we see nothing. We want to see the compassion that we've grown accustomed to, but His face seems to be made of stone at these times. This doesn't mean that He has quit loving us. At these times we need to recall what He has told us or shown us during those times of intimate communication. He hasn't moved away. He's still just as close and just as much in love with us as He was when we were on the mountain top with Him. Maybe He's trying to see what we are going to do with information or direction He has already given us. Maybe He's got us on stand by while He gets someone or something else ready so that we can continue with our part of His Master Plan.

I don't know what it is for you. To be honest with you, way too often, I don't know what it is for me either. I stare into the clouds waiting for some sort of sign of what to do, what to say and I don't hear nor see anything. At those times we must do the task in front of us. Whatever it may be, do what is in front of you. If we need direction or correction our Father will take care of that. When a child learns to walk, for a while we may say, "good step, now take another one", but after a while we only comment when correction or direction is needed.

Are you in this place? Feeling like you're walking alone and wanting something, anything from God. Keep walking. No matter how impassive we think His face looks, He still loves us just as much as He always did. His desire to fellowship with us hasn't diminished. Find out if there is something in your life that has caused a line to be drawn between you and God. If so, deal with it. If not, wait and see what His next word, His next direction, His next correction is for you. Don't let the silence fool you. If you're His, He has something for you. You want to know how I know this? Because you're still here. If God was finished with you or me, and had nothing else for us to do, He'd call us home because this world is not our home. Find out what you are here for, what to do, who to pray for or help in other ways. Don't give up. His love doesn't.

CAN I HAVE YOUR ATTENTION PLEASE?

"It happened that while Jesus was praying in a certain place, after He had finished, one of His disciples said to Him, "Lord, teach us to pray just as John also taught his disciples. And He said to them, When you pray, say: Father, hallowed be Your name. Your kingdom come."

Luke 11:1-2 (New American Standard Bible)

You know how people and other living things learn things that you actually wish they had not learned? Small children learn how to talk, how to walk, and when they get older, how to drive a car and to manipulate parents. Early on little girls learn how to wrap their fathers around their "pinky". OK, I'm talking about me in the last sentence. People learn things that, just because they can do them, doesn't necessarily mean you really want them to do them.

Here's how this relates to Biscuit and Catfish. Biscuit, long ago, taught himself that if he wants my attention he will come up to me while I'm sitting down and "nose butt" my hand. If that doesn't work, he'll do it again. If that doesn't work, he'll jump up on the side of my chair and scratch at me as if to say in his own cute little way, "CAN I HAVE YOU ATTENTION PLEASE?" This may have to do with food, water, going outside, riding in the car, whatever he desires at the moment, he wants my attention now. He has learned that persistence usually wins over resistance. Here's the problem, he's taught this to Catfish too.

I know that to you this might not sound like a problem, but let us remember, Biscuit about thirty five pounds, Catfish about sixty five to seventy pounds. See the situation? Biscuit nose butts and it's kind of cute. Catfish does it and both the chair and I could wind up upside down on the floor. Linebackers are more subtle with their "quarterback etiquette". The running of the bulls in Pamplona is more genteel than Catfish when he wants your attention. Usually my response is no, no, no. . .yes. Again, the persistence pays off.

Not that God is as immovable as I am with Biscuit and Catfish, but sometimes. . . OK, I'm pretty movable, but whatever. God though wants to see our dedication, our commitment, to our request of Him. Is this something that we are approaching Him in passion or in passing? Are we serious or is this just something that sounded good to us at the moment?

God is what's called immutable, never changing, but not immovable. He is moved to compassion by what goes on with His children all of the time. The difference is, He knows that this, whatever this is, is going to be a problem long before we would, and He dealt with it then. He has no horizons. He saw it coming and put something in place before we ever knew that there would be a problem, let alone seeing the problem itself.

We don't pray to get God's attention. Now hear this because it's going to be a bit confusing, we pray to get OUR attention, to get our focus focused. We pray to keep ourselves rightly focused. God doesn't sleep. If He did, we might have to wake Him up to get His attention. God is omniscient, all knowing. If not, we'd have to bring Him up to speed on our situation. God is omnipresent, all places simultaneously. If He weren't, we'd have to wait until He was in the neighborhood to get with us.

Are you serious about what you're asking God? Have you done your part, or are you just sitting on your amazing grace and expecting Him to do everything; give you the desire, the direction, the where with all, the oomph to do what needs to be done?

You always have His attention; today, tonight, tomorrow.........right now.

CATFISH AND CHRISTMAS, A TERROR IN TINSEL.

"For unto you is born this day in the city of David a Saviour, which is Christ the Lord."

Luke 2:11 (King James Version)

As we approach Christmas fear grips me. No, its not the shopping, malls like cattle cars, happy store clerks imploding because the "swiper" on the credit card machine didn't work. (Remember when you use to buy something, people rang it up on a cash register and you gave them money?) Yes kids, the green stuff came long before the plastic stuff. Ari once told Elain and me that we must have money, we had checks. No, no, no, that's not the way it works. But forgive me, I digress.

It's not all these things that strike fear in me, it's this. This will be Catfish's first Christmas and he is destructive. Only today, I came home, found one of the massive pillows from the sofa, about as big as a Volkswagon, on the floor and chewed on. He had dragged if off the sofa, thrown it to the ground, knocked over a T.V. tray which almost hit the front of the entertainment center (with a glass front) with the television and stereo on it.

What does this have to do with Christmas you say? The Christmas Tree. Yes, you know the thing that you go out and either cut down and kill yourself or allow someone else to do it for you and you pay them. Either way, we diminish our forests in the true "spirit of the season." Back to Catfish and the tree. Again, he is destructive. He destroys pillows, furniture, stuffed animals (there is stuffed squirrel shrapnel all over the house). We even find parts and pieces of trees from our back yard in the house from time to time. You get the picture?

Now imagine our beautiful Christmas Tree. We always cut our own. Yes, a real tree, not one of those sacrilegious fake things with purple lights or swans on it, a real, green, have to water it every day, Christmas Tree. I might add, with ornaments dating back to Ari's pre-school days. By the way, want a neat tradition for your family? Buy a new Christmas ornament every year. Not the typical stuff advertised, but rather get something wherever you have traveled or someplace where you and your family have had a good time. We have such things as chile peppers from San Antonio and a Macy's Star from New York. Its really a fun thing to remember the stories behind the ornaments.

Back to the tree. You now have this picture in your mind? Beautiful tree, filled with ornaments and decorations that mean a great deal to us, presents underneath, stuffed animals (remember the shrapnel) and other decorations around the house. Enter Catfish.

First, I've been around him outside, I've seen what he does to trees as soon as he goes outside, he waters them. Water and electricity, not a good mix. Next we have the presents with their pretty paper and bows, perfect for tearing up and "confettiing" around the house to celebrate the Yuletide. Again, remember the stuffed animals and their fates? Elain and Ari have about one million Christmas stuffed animals. Often times I have had to move out during Christmas Season because there wasn't enough room for all of the stuffed toys and me. To make a long story not so long, I know too late, you see my fears, and there are many.

Let's look at Someone else who could have had fears of how His Christmas present was treated. What we actually celebrate at Christmas is the birth of Our Lord and Savior Jesus Christ. That may come as a shock to some of you, but yes, that's the true reason for the celebration. What if Our Father in Heaven had looked down on us, seen how we were, and said, "why should I send Someone this valuable to them? They'll just destroy Him"? Interesting question, huh? What if God just figured, why waste My Son on a bunch of destructive people who would rather mess up than be right?

Do you see the picture? Our family will spend hours and dollars, buying a Christmas Tree, transporting it home, decorating it, rearranging the house and then throw it out when we are through with it. God sent us His One and Only Son for our present. Not to give us something shiny to play with, but rather to save us from spending eternity without Him. What do we do? Too often, we decorate, play with, celebrate for a while and then....throw Him out when we don't want to play any more.

What about you this Christmas? Does the Father need to be fearful with what you are going to do with the Present He has sent you? Will you treat Him with the value and honor He deserves or will you treat Him like a new toy, one that you play with for a while and then toss aside? Its up to you, but remember this, no matter what you do, how you treat Him, He is still so much in love with you that He set aside His royalty in Heaven, came down here in the form of an infant in a manger with absolutely no rights or privileges, for but one reason. Us! To reconcile us to the Father. Make this Christmas special for you, your family on Earth, and your family in Heaven. Treat the most magnificent Present ever presented with all the praise, worship and glory He deserves. He's given Himself to you, why don't you give yourself to Him?

Oh, and by the way, pray for us and Catfish. The Tree is up and he has a wicked grin on his face.

THE DAY CATFISH WAS BEATEN UP BY A STUFFED ANIMAL.

He ransoms me unharmed from the battle waged against me, even though many oppose me.

Psalm 55:18 (New International Version)

We have quite a few stuffed animals around my house. No, we don't have small children; and no, Ari, Elain and I don't collect them. What we do have are two mutton-headed puppies who like to play with them (translate, *tear them up*). You can't walk through the living room without stepping on, tripping on, or kicking one of the 8 million toys that Biscuit and Catfish play with. But that's fine. As with any child that you love, you put up with some of the clutter. What I want to tell you about is the day that one of them beat up Catfish.

It was a day like any other day. The sun was shining, birds were singing, and God was in His Heaven. Biscuit was meditating (that's sleeping, in pastor talk); and Catfish was playing because that's what Catfish does. Suddenly I saw Catfish flip over and yelp like he had been attacked by a bear. I looked at him in time to see a stuffed squirrel (how embarrassing) on top of him, and him squirming like he was trying to rescue himself from the clutches of an 8-armed, 800-pound monster. I just had to stop and laugh. Catfish weighs in at about 70 pounds. The killer stuffed squirrel weighed in at about 10 ounces…that's *ounces*. But there they were, Catfish on the bottom screaming like death was chasing him with a stick, and the stuffed squirrel on top, thinking whatever stuffed squirrels think. Maybe the squirrel was getting even for all the times Catfish had left him outside in the rain.

This episodic adventure was hilarious to watch when it was Catfish and a toy. It is not, however, so funny when it's us. "I've never let a stuffed animal get the best of me," you may say. Maybe not, but I'll guarantee you that you and I have let things "spook" us that shouldn't have. I was told that the water content in 8 blocks of fog is around a glass full. Not very much, is it? But we still get uneasy when we are in fog, though, don't we? I read that 90 percent of the issues we worry about are those we can't do anything about anyway. Now don't get me wrong, I'm not telling you to not be concerned about situations in life; and I'm not telling you to not be prepared for them. What I *am* telling you is to remember that a stuffed squirrel can't beat you up. The biggest reason for this is that you and I are not alone. First and foremost, we have God in our corner. The Scripture says, "when the storms come" (Proverbs 1:27), not *if* the storms come. Isn't it good to know that the battle is God's, not yours? Secondly, He has given us a group of fellow believers called the church to help us through hard times. Regardless of the definition of "hard times," God says that both He and the church will be there for you.

Your part? Take His hand. Don't belong to a church? Why not? Why wouldn't you want to be around people who will care and help? If you haven't found that place, don't give up. It's out there. Where I'm going is this: You can't fight the battles alone. The more you try, the more tired you get. Soon enough--too soon--your strength will fail. It's funny to watch Catfish wrestle with stuffed squirrels. It's even funnier when the squirrel wins. It's not so funny, however, when it's us. Just remember, you are not alone. "I will never leave you, nor forsake you" (Hebrews 13:5).

———————— ————————

CATFISH DOESN'T HAVE A REVERSE

"In Him we have redemption through His blood, the forgiveness of our trespasses, according to the riches of His grace which He lavished on us."

Ephesians 1:7-8 (New American Standard Bible)

That's right, Catfish doesn't know how to turn around. Oh, I'm not saying that he never backs up but when he starts to do something it seems that he will go through a wall rather than turn around and go another way.

The other day Elain was sitting on the sofa and Catfish got at her feet and decided to climb up her leg to the top of her head and then get behind her on the sofa cushions. For those of you unaware, Catfish weighs about 70 pounds but thinks he's a teacup Catahoula Cur. That's the state dog of Louisiana where we live. Get this picture, my bride is sitting there minding her own business and along comes the "galoot". With a smile on his face, he starts up her leg holding own as best he can with those five pound hams at the end of his legs that we call feet. Up to her lap he goes, then straddled across her diagonally with rear feet on the sofa on her right side and front feet with freight train head over her left shoulder on the back cushions of the sofa. Hold on, it gets even better. Next he decides to climb around her head and shoulders and rest himself on said cushions like he's some sort of fur stole on Elain's neck and shoulders. In typical fashion the decision to stay there lasts for almost a minute and he struggles to remove himself from that situation and almost takes Elain's head with him. Where upon Elain almost takes his head as a trophy. All in all it was fun to watch, not so much to be involved in. I had to walk a fine line and make sure that I laughed at Catfish's antics and not Elain's discomfort.

Too often we find ourselves in the same predicament. We won't or don't feel we can reverse ourselves. We get ourselves into situations and feel that for some reason or another, be it pride, ignorance or hard-headedness, we bull ahead only making the matter worse. It could be the misunderstanding with our spouse, the disagreement with a parent or child, the person at work or school that we are at odds with.

Let me ask you a question, have you ever won an argument? I'm not talking about some sort of educational debate where one needed to be right to make the point of the whatever the discussion was supposed to be, I'm talking about you and someone else arguing about something or other where there can't be a winner because even if you win, what have you won? This is what I'm talking about, you argue, put someone in their place and now you don't like them and they don't like you, what have you won? Now two people don't speak to each other, don't like each other, don't respect each other, ain't that wonderful? We get ourselves into situations and feel we have no option except to "bull" ahead and ram our way through when in reality if we were to reverse ourselves everyone, including self, would be much happier.

You have an option today, not only with the people around you but also with God. You've boxed yourself into a corner. You think that there's no way out. You've sinned beyond any forgiveness that can ever be given. Wrong!! I always think of Peter here. Not wise mature Peter but loudmouthed brash young Peter, you know, "me and You Jesus no matter what the rest do, it's me and You". When he made that statement, which I very much paraphrased there, it was mere hours before the man who said this, who had literally walked with Jesus for about three years denied him not once, not twice but three times. And not to someone with sword to his throat but a women in a courtyard. And guess what, not only did Jesus forgive him, He still used him mightily in the building of His church.

Here's your choice, bull on ahead and make yourself and others around miserable or turn around—it's called repenting. Turning from your sin and to God. Don't try to win the argument. What have you won? If it's with a person, you're now at odds with one another. If it's with God you're estranged from Him and that is most assuredly a place you don't want to be.

What stands between you and your Heavenly Father today? He not only can wipe it out like it never happened, He wants to. All He's waiting on is for you to ask. Don't be like Catfish. With him it's funny to watch him try to get out of something without help. With us, it's just dumb. Especially when we have One Who is both able and available to help us turn around and go in reverse.

CATFISH REPENTS WITH THE BEST OF THEM

"But God demonstrates His own love toward us, in that while we were yet sinners, Christ died for us."
Romans 5:8 (New American Standard Bible)

As I gaze out into our back yard, something catches my eye. Not the day lilies that are starting to bloom. Not the trees that are starting to have beautiful purple blossoms on them in the spring time. Not even Biscuit and Catfish sunning themselves in the late winter sun on a beautiful day. No, what catches my attention is the swimming pool that Catfish is digging for us in the back yard where plants used to be. Not only has he turned the yard into "the land of a thousand lakes", now he's making one of them the size of the Grand Canyon. What used to be a well kempt pretty yard is now the playground for two four legged destruction machines. They run and play in bushes that this time last year were full and lush. This year they look like scarecrows because the two of them run in and out through them. There is a beaten down path along the flower bed around the back part of the house which is where Biscuit and Catfish do their ever vigilant patrol morning, noon, and night. Along the fence between our's and our neighbor's yard, all of the lilies are beaten down because our two mutts and Scooter next door run back and forth, back and forth barking and protecting us from whatever it is they are protecting us from. Get the picture? Not exactly the landscaping I thought I wanted when I moved to suburbia. Where once was flora and fauna, now is "ye old swimming hole". This doesn't make me joyous.

So, are we all on the same page here? Do we understand that Catfish has done something here worthy of incurring my wrath? Perhaps some correction is due here? I can just see all of your nodding your heads right along with me here. The Big Fish has done wrong and deserves to be punished. So I must do so.

I walk out of the back door onto the porch, catch him excavating the area where he has decided to put the pool, its important that you catch them in the act, and with love and gentleness I bellow his name just to make sure that I have his attention. I do. Head drops. Tail goes between his legs. Are you familiar with the phrase "hurt dog look"? This is what I see, drooping brown eyes and a look of remorse that would work except that I've seen it a few hundred times, remember the fertilizer on the carpet?

CATFISH, COME HERE. I make a strong suggestion to him that he should come into my presence to discuss the placing of the deck chairs around the pool area. Now here is the part that really surprised me, he came. I fully expected him to run away, hide, point to Biscuit and say, "I was fixing this hole that Biscuit dug, aren't you proud of me? Let's kill him". But no, he didn't. He came to me; head down, tail down, hurt dog look, remorse in all of his body language. He knew that he had done wrong and that punishment was due. Swift retribution, a condemning tone, loud words, perhaps even a newspaper, all it really takes is one page rolled up, to the part that clears the fence last. He came to me.

Slowly he walked up, straight to me, put his head and shoulders between my legs as if to get in my lap and sat down. I melted. He had played me like a cheap fiddle. I couldn't punish him. He was so trusting, so ready to receive richly deserved punishment that I knew that he knew that he had done wrong and was totally sorry for his actions and would never do this again. Right. Well I did berate him for a while and told him that what he did was wrong. He swore an oath to me that this would never happen again. Once again, right. I know it will indeed happen again. Do you know why? It's in his nature to dig holes. That's just who he is. He is of the breed of dog that digs. Some do, some don't, he do.

It is in our nature to do wrong. We have that propensity to rebel in us. We do wrong. The Scriptural term for it is sin. We sin. But here's the great news. God forgives. As long as we truly repent, turn from, and go to Him when He calls us to look at that sin and denounce it, God will forgive us.

Have you been digging holes in the back yard? With all my heart I hope not because if you have we've now discovered a whole new set of problems for you. But you know what I mean. We all do it. We say the wrong thing, do the wrong thing, think the wrong thing. We sin. But the Great Gift is this, Jesus paid for all of that sin in full. No matter what we've done, no matter what we do, Christ has paid for that and all we have to do is come to our Heavenly Father, ask His forgiveness and He will give it. Not based on our remorse, but based on the fact that His Son paid in full for that sin in advance of our committing it. This is truly Good News.

Whatever you think stands between you and the instantaneous forgiveness our Father has ready for you is false and weaker than His love and forgiveness for you. Go. No, don't just go, run to Him. If you have to with head down, tail between your legs, remorse in your heart, whatever it takes, run to Him. His arms are open wide. He has true, unchanging un-diminishing love just waiting for you. There may be consequences involved, but I promise, it won't be as bad as the consequences you'll suffer without Him.

Well, I've got to go to my back yard now. The Catfish Memorial Swimming Pool needs filling in and I get to do it while he lies down, eats a treat and watches. Sometimes life isn't fair. It wasn't for Jesus. But He took the unfairness, a criminal's death on the cross, so that you and I wouldn't have to face what we deserved. Unfairness meted out on the Only Begotten Son of God just for us. Aren't you glad? I know I am.

─────────── ───────────

CATFISH'S SPECIAL HOUSE

"I was glad when they said unto me, let us go into the house of the Lord."

Psalm 122:1 (New American Standard)

In other stories I have eluded to the fact that Catfish is not the most "attention free" being around our household. As a matter of fact, he's the least. Even compared with our daughter, Ari, (who was Arianne until she grew up and became Ari) and her involvement in the Miss America pageant system, Catfish is still more high maintenance. How, you ask? I'm glad you did. You see, there would be no story if you didn't. How? Because he is the most destructive creature I've ever been around. Not mean mind you, but still destructive. Godzilla on his worst day doesn't hold a candle to Catfish. Hurricanes, monsoons, earthquakes bow in respect to the destructive power of Catfish, the Master of Destruction. Once again, how, you ask. He chews. What does he chew? Whatever is in front of him. Food, the dish its in, paper, plastic, furniture, all fall prey to the jaws of iron. He has even gotten into a storage room and chewed open and spread about fifty pound bags of dirt and rocks (it looked pretty cool, but it needed to be outside and not on the floor of a storage room). A sofa has met his wrath, Elain's favorite chair, one of my Bibles (one third of the Gospel of John has really been treated as food for thought by Catfish) has been devoured by the bottomless pit. I would keep waiting to drive into our driveway one day and find the house gone and Catfish sitting in a vacant lot with a smile on his face and an extended belly from the feast of our entire home in him.

Do you see the problem? Well, there are solutions. One, get rid of him. We can't do that, we love him too much. Two, dog training. Good idea, but he ate the trainer. Three, a muzzle. It just flat didn't work. And finally four, his "special" house. What is his special house? A kennel. Don't tell him though, he thinks he has his own apartment. We have to put him in there every time we leave the house. Ten minutes or five hours, it makes no difference, Catfish has to go in his special house. He doesn't mind though. As a matter of fact, after the second time of going in there, he stands at the door of it when we go to leave knowing that he is going to get a treat when he goes in and that he won't be in trouble when we get back. Let me tell you, Catfish can grovel with the best of them when he has done wrong. Don't let people tell you dogs are dumb and don't know when they have done wrong, they do. Both Catfish and Biscuit know when we walk in the door and they've done wrong they either hide or try to blend in with the floor or furniture. They know. Don't let them kid you, they know. Which brings me to an interesting thought. If dogs are so dumb, then how is it that they are fed, housed, doctored and generally taken care of at someone else's time and expense? I don't know about you but Biscuit and Catfish don't go out at my convenience, I let them out when they want to go out and back in when they want to come back in. Who has who trained?

Anyhow, the special house. Catfish knows that he goes there and one of the things that it does is keep him out of trouble. It is also a place that we have fixed up with blankets, treats and toys. It is his place of comfort to go to. We have a place to go to likewise that can keep us out of trouble and be a place of warmth and comfort. It's called the presence of God. Now a simpler way to put this and a more understandable place to go is this, church. If the churches in your area are doing what they are supposed to be doing and being what they are supposed to be, they indeed are a place where you can go to be comforted and kept warm. The church should be a place where you can learn how to stay out of trouble and be with our heavenly Father and learn what He wants and expects from His children. Church does not make Him more God, He is God and that is that, but rather the Church should show us how we can draw closer to Him and be everything He wants us to be and have the relationship with Him that He designed us to have. Picture getting clearer? We don't go to church for God. He won't limp if we don't show up. We go so that we can receive all that He has for us. Not stuff, but rather the joy, peace, wisdom, rest, knowledge, kindness, and on and on and on that He wants for us to make us complete that we can only get in His presence. How do I know this? I've seen God work in the lives of so many including myself and my family.

Now if you are in a church and you aren't receiving all that God has for you, the first thing you need to do is ask why. Is it me? Hard question.

I'll have to be honest with you, most of the time I have found that too many people want God to be committed to them on a full time basis and them be committed to God on a part-time basis at best. We treat God like a soda machine, when I want a soda I put in a dollar and get my drink, when I don't, I just walk on by. He's not that way. If you'll check in the Gospels you'll find that when Jesus called the disciples, with each one of them the call was simply "follow me" and the "follow me" that Jesus was saying is not a part time thing.

Find a place and a time that is special to you. That church, that prayer time, that reading time that will make a difference in you. You see, we don't want Catfish to be in trouble with us. We want to love on him, give him treats, play with him. God wants to love on you, bless you and have fellowship with you, but if you're disobedient He can't. He has to discipline His children in order for them to be what He created them for. Catfish is catching on, why don't you?

CUTE IS THE ONLY THING THAT KEEP HIM ALIVE

"BLESSED ARE THOSE WHOSE LAWLESS DEEDS HAVE BEEN FORGIVEN, AND WHOSE SINS HAVE BEEN COVERED. BLESSED IS THE MAN WHOSE SIN THE LORD WILL NOT TAKE INTO ACCOUNT."
Romans 4:7-8 (New American Standard Bible)

Catfish is a living, breathing, walking, eating, destroying being whose only purpose on this planet, it seems, is to drive me, Elain, and Ari nuts. He tears up, throws about, bounces off of furniture, and doesn't have nearly the respect for flooring that the rest of us do. We talk among ourselves often and say that "cute is the only thing that keeps him alive."

Despite all he does, does wrong, and tears up, we still love him. Oh, we punish and correct sometimes, but we never stop loving him. Give him up? Take him back? Nope, not going to happen. He's ours, and we love him. Even if he ran away, we would still be ours and we would still love him. It would have to be he who ran away from us, we would never run away from him.

Now I want you to ask yourself something. Considering that we are made in God's image, aren't we, to a degree, "cute" to Him? I know that I'm kind of stretching here, but if you think about it, His image would not be ugly. I'm not talking about sandy blonde hair, dashing blue eyes, and a disarming smile that just makes you feel the sun shine. Seriously, I don't know what God looks like on the outside, but on the "inside" He has all of the attributes that He wants to pass along to us through His Son, Jesus–attributes such as mercy (II Corinthians 1:3), love (I John 4:16), patience (Romans 15:5), and kindness (Titus 3:4).

Despite how much we mess up, tear up, and do wrong, God still loves us. He so wants us to be made in the image of His Son that He gives us chance after chance. He actually sees us in the image of Jesus because He *can* (remember, He has eternal eyes). He sees us not as we are in our fallen state, but as we will be in our perfect or complete state. If you want to call it cute, go ahead. God seeing us as cute, seeing us as perfect through the blood of His Son, may be the only thing that keeps us alive.

DON'T DRINK THE MUDDY WATER

"You prepare a table before me in the presence of my enemies:" Psalm 23:5
(New American Standard Bible)

We keep Biscuit and Catfish's water dish on the screened covered patio. Don't worry, they aren't going to die of thirst. I should be treated so well. We do this because Catfish can slurp water and somehow get more on his face than in his face. This in turn becomes a wet spot that is streamed throughout the house until his face quits leaking. Now I know that our floors are not hallowed ground, but if Catfish gets them wet, I get sacrificed. You guys understand, don't you fellows? We stand there with a goofy look on our faces, our shoulders shrugged, and "Baby, I'm sorry" pouring from our lips in the best innocent voice we can muster, because somehow someway, this is my fault. I don't need proof. I don't even need an explanation. I just know it is

I remember walking outside with Biscuit and Catfish to go outside, get water and "romp". Their water dish was both low and not too appealing looking. I picked it up, took it inside, washed it out and added clean fresh water. As Biscuit and Catfish watched me, I took it onto the patio and put it down for them. Now please understand, this thing holds enough water to fill up a steam locomotive so there was more than enough for both of them. Biscuit started drinking. Catfish on the other hand, immediately walked past it, into the back yard and started drinking from a mud puddle that he was also standing in which only helped it to get dirtier.

We do exactly the same thing. Our Father sets a banquet table for us, we walk by it ignoring both the banquet table and Him and head directly for the mud puddle that is no good for us. No I'm not talking about fast food. I admit, I am a serious partaker of fine cuisine from a Styrofoam box. I'm talking about rather than partaking of the good that God has for us, we gorge on the good enough (or so we think), or the rotten that the world has for us. By the way, about that good thing, the enemy of the best is not the worst, it's the "good enough". We can spot the worst many times, but too often we settle for good enough.

Why do we bypass God's banquet and head for the mud puddle? Good question. Perhaps we don't feel we're good enough? You're right, but we don't go there on our goodness, but rather the goodness of Jesus. Perhaps we don't recognize the goodness of the banquet? Understandable. Then learn of it. You see, the banquet doesn't represent food for the body as much as it is food for life, not what we need to exist, but rather what we need to really live. Just as our bodies won't remain healthy on a diet of "to go" boxes, our lives, our souls won't stay healthy on a diet of garbage the world tries to foist on us.

Quit being thick headed. God went through an ordeal and effort for us to have that banquet. As a matter of fact, He created us to partake of the banquet with Him. He sacrificed His One and Only Son to get us out of the muddy water. What else can we ask for? Pay attention. As we say in the South, "show some smarts". Come to the table. Jesus has written the invitation for you in His own blood.

––––––––––––––– –––––––––––––––

DON'T WORRY, BE CATFISH

"Rejoice in the Lord always; again I will say, rejoice!"
Philippians 4:4 (New American Standard Bible)

Have you ever heard the song, "Don't Worry, Be Happy"? If you're familiar with the song, you know that it speaks of not carrying the cares of the world. It suggests, in fact, that the best way to deal with adversity is to stay positive—that is, "don't worry, be happy." Sorry, I know that phrase may be stuck in your brain now, but that's really not so bad. When I watch Catfish, who has the "don't worry, be happy" lifestyle down to a science, I know there's a lot to recommend it.

The other day I watched Catfish outside as he loped, bounded, wrestled with a stick (the stick won), chased a leaf (it was a tie), and just generally had a great time with who he was and where he was. Why do you suppose he was able to do this? First, he's a dog and doesn't have reasoning skills. But from a deeper perspective, what does he have to worry about? His daddy (that would be me) takes care of him, feeds him, puts a roof over his head, clothes him (well, not literally, but I do keep him clean and groomed), take care of him when he's sick, love on him constantly … so what does he have to be concerned about?

About the only time I see Catfish unhappy is when he's done something wrong while Elain, Ari and I were away. When we come back, he hides under the kitchen table because he knows "trouble's a'coming"; and, even then, all he usually gets is a good finger-pointing and a stern voice calling him Rot-Ten. (This is generally done by Elain or Ari; I'm the "good cop.")

What burdens are you carrying today that you really shouldn't be carrying? Worries are bigger than you; therefore, you need your Father's help to overcome them. Besides, a statistic I read indicates that most (80 to 90 percent) of what we worry about will never happen. So what has you "spooked"? Can *you* fix it? Look to the same Father who takes care of you, feeds you, puts a roof over your head, clothes you, and wants to love on you. He will help you with this problem, too. God may have a part for us to do in it, maybe something to learn--or He may just want to take care of it for you and you're standing in the way.

Whatever it is, look to Him. He wants to--and can--help you in any matter. If we have the attitude of trust with Him that we should, we could be like Catfish much more often. Go outside, lope, bound about, chase a leaf. Don't worry, be Catfish.

HE BIT ME

"Know that the LORD, He is God; It is He who has made us, and not we ourselves; We are His people and the sheep of His pasture. Enter into His gates with thanksgiving, And into His courts with praise. Be thankful to Him, and bless His name. For the LORD is good; His mercy is everlasting, And His truth endures to all generations.

Psalm 100:3-5 (New King James Version)

The other day I was playing with Biscuit and Catfish and Catfish bit me. Not too hard, but a definite bite. It made me think. Everything they have came from me. Catfish can't give me food; it's my food. He can't give me his bed, which by the way in the past few days, he has eaten. Have you ever seen a room filled with foam rubber confetti? I would be afraid for his stomach, but its so much fun to watch him jump off of furniture now because he bounces so well.

Anyway. Doctor bills, dog collars, toys, all from me. So what can he do for me? Just love me. That's all. I don't want or need anything from either Catfish or Biscuit. Everything they have came from me. I just want their love.

All we have came from God. Your job, money. . .Wait a minute you say, I made that money myself! Who gave you the ability to do your work? Who gave you the ability to breathe for that matter? Your house, clothes, all your possessions came from God. Too often we not only love things and use people when we should be loving people and using things, we bite the hand of the very One Who enabled us to have the things we have.

Have you said thank you to God today? If you're able to read this you owe God a thank you. If someone is reading it to you, you owe God a thank you. We can't give Him anything that He doesn't already have. We can't bribe Him, threaten Him, or treat Him like He owes us. Just thank Him and love Him as He has first loved you.

---- ----

HE KNOWS MY VOICE

"Come to Me, all who are weary and heavy-laden, and I will give you rest."

Matthew 11:28 (New American Standard Bible)

I've told you before that Biscuit is just about the best "commear" dog I've ever had. Catfish, on the other hand, is not. I can remember the first time that Biscuit came to me outside when I called him. I would have bought him a car if he had asked for it. As it was I was eager to find any treat that I could give him to show my appreciation in a way that he understood. Catfish has just not caught on to "commear". He stares, he wags, he grins, he does cute puppy things, but he doesn't come when I call. Biscuit is by my side in a heartbeat when he hears my voice. Catfish, on the other hand, is not.

It's not really that Catfish is that big a dunce, ok, yes he is, but it's really because he doesn't know my voice as well as Biscuit. You see, Biscuit and I have a history. He has more time of knowing and learning my voice. He has a greater understanding of the love and kindnesses I want to shower on him. Why? He's been around longer and has built a loving relationship with me through years of each other's company. Catfish, on the other hand, has not. He still wants to run in the street, in the backyard at midnight, through the house, and wherever else he can successfully make me crazy. But, with time, he and I will draw closer together and have the relationship that Biscuit and I have. He'll learn to let me love on him, lavish him with blessings and take care of him as I have Biscuit. I want that to happen, but this is more up to him than me.

How's your relationship with God? Do you know His voice when He calls you? Why not? Could it be because you haven't spent enough time listening FOR Him and listening TO Him? There are those times when He calls you to correct you, but most of the time it's because He just wants to be with you and love on you. He even tells us, "Come to Me all of you who are weary and heavy laden, and I will give you rest." (Matthew 11:28)

What are you waiting for, God to have to chase you through the bushes at midnight because you don't know His voice? Biscuit knows the love of his father and gets the benefits of that knowledge. Catfish, on the other hand, doesn't and he misses out on a lot of blessings. Don't be like Catfish, learn your Father's voice, run to Him and receive His blessings.

——————————— ———————————

HE SPEAKS TO US HOW WE'LL UNDERSTAND

> "Then he was told, "Go, stand on the mountain at attention before God. God will pass by. A hurricane wind ripped through the mountains and shattered the rocks before God, but God wasn't to be found in the wind; after the wind an earthquake, but God wasn't in the earthquake; and after the earthquake fire, but God wasn't in the fire; and after the fire a gentle and quiet whisper."
>
> **1 Kings 19:11-12 (The Message)**

Recently Ari, our daughter, and I took both Biscuit and Catfish to the vet's office. Did you hear me, BOTH Biscuit and Catfish. This was as much a thrill as it is to nail Jello to the wall. Biscuit loves riding in the car, he was all over the place trying to get in, run around, jump in our laps, drive the car, all the things he loves to do. Catfish, on the other hand, believes that the car is the rolling box of death. I've seen people walking to the "hangin' tree" on cowboy movies with more joy than Catfish takes with him to get in the car. He lays on the back seat, doesn't move or even look at us. He actually tries to bury his head in the crack of the car seat. When we do see his face when he comes up for air, he looks at us as if to say "how can you do this to me?" All the while, Biscuit thinks he is at the amusement park. All he needs is cotton candy and a soft drink and he's happy as can be.

As we pulled up to our vet's office, both remembered with their little doggie memories where we were and let us know that they were not happy to be there. They both knew that this was the place where needles and toe nail clippings abounded and not a haven of happiness. Biscuit had put on about five pounds so we changed his name to Round Boy and Catfish, well he's just Catfish, happy to be anyplace other than the car.

Overall they were both fine. We took them outside on their separate leashes so that they might christen the flower beds and plants around

Dr. Perry's office as is the custom. He doesn't mind, we've known him for about twenty years and he remembers all of our dog children by their names. Actually, as you probably know, neither Biscuit nor Catfish know that they're dogs. They think they are humans without thumbs and therefore are set apart and live on a plane above the rest of us mere mortals who spend our lives working and walking upright.

Anyhow, as we went to get in the car, Catfish remembered the rolling box of death and decided he had ridden enough for the day. Ari had him on his leash and he pulled backwards out of his collar, leash and all. They were behind me so I saw nothing, only heard Ari screaming at both Catfish and me to do what ever it was daddies do. Please understand, we weren't mad at him, we were scared to death. Doc's office is about thirty feet from a busy road and we had pictures of Catfish running into the street and getting hit by a car. However, when we yelled it only scared him more and he dropped to the ground. All he wanted to do was get away from the situation and the yelling voices from people he loved and who he thought loved him, yet they weren't speaking to him in the way he was accustomed. Ari and I realized what was going on, we lowered our voices. Catfish stayed slunked to the ground, but stopped when he heard his people talking to him in the voice and tone he understood. We got him in the car, loved on him for a while and then headed home.

This made me think. God probably doesn't speak to us in His "God Voice" because we couldn't handle it. If he spoke to us with a voice that thundered from the heavens we would drop to the ground and try to get away. Now here's the problem--if He's trying to tell us something that is going to keep us from harm and we run because we are afraid of His voice, we could be harmed because we didn't understand what nor why He was talking to us that way. This is why God speaks to us in ways that we understand. We understand circumstances. We understand a quiet voice, even though its easy to ignore. We understand, in part, the Scriptures. He speaks to us adapting His tone to our ears, His Words to our understanding. It is my opinion that communications is on the shoulders of the communicator. Our Father doesn't want to be some cosmic mystery to us. He wants His children to understand when he corrects, warns, teaches and says " I love you". Don't be afraid of His voice. Listen for what He is saying to you. It may be something that He has for no one else, but we must listen.

I KNEW IT WAS RAINING, CATFISH DIDN'T

"But if any of you lacks wisdom, let him ask of God, who gives to all generously and without reproach, and it will be given to him."

James 1:5 (New American Standard Bible)

The other day I was sitting where I sit, doing what I do, so you can read what I write. (That was a long journey for a short trip wasn't it?) Anyway, Catfish was bugging the daylights out of me to go outside and when he does that, I run, not walk, to the back patio door because this usually means he needs to use the bathroom and when he needs to use the bathroom, the only question is "where". Inside, outside it really doesn't matter that much Dad, your choice. (He's really not that bad any more, I was just pretending).

However, I looked at him and on the inside said, "you really don't want to go outside, its raining". But one doesn't argue with one's dog because that makes one look real stupid. So I went to the door opened it stepped onto our patio, (you didn't think I was going to stand in the rain did you?) and he strolled out with me. As he heard and saw the rain he turned back to me as if to say, "Did you know it was raining"? I looked back at him as if to say, "Yup". You see it was like this, I knew that he really didn't want to go where he thought he wanted to go. I knew that it was pouring outside and that he wouldn't like to go there. We do that a lot. We think that we want to do something and God tells us through people, circumstances, conscience, Scripture, "you really don't want to go there, or you really don't want to do that". Unfortunately, entirely too often, we brush His hand aside and charge off to pour our energies and our beings into something that is not only a waste of time, but an endangerment to ourselves and our relationship with God.

The next time, why don't you check with God before you follow the crowd, grab for the brass ring, jump through the hoop, or whatever it is that looks bright and shiny that moment. He'll give you direction as to whether or not you're going to get "rained on" or not.

As for Catfish, he got wet, I dried him off, and we waited till it quit with the downpour to go outside and the carpet was kept from getting watered for another day.

--- ---

IF CATFISH DOES IT HIS WAY, HE MESSES UP

Jesus answered, "I am the way and the truth and the life. No one comes to the Father except through me."

John 14:6 (New International Version)

I love spending time with Catfish. He's just so full of life. He bounces and jumps when he's around you. He seems to keep a smile on his face all the time. He always wants to play with me and cuddle with me. He just has a great personality and generally speaking is a joy to be around. One thing he does sometimes really spoils the mood and does so quickly. Sometimes he wants to jump up to me and hang on to me. He jumps up to me, puts his ten pound hams-paws on either side of me and digs into me with his claws. When he does this he isn't being mean, he's just trying the best way he knows to get to me. But what it does is hurt me and I get that flare of anger, yes ministers get angry too. Sometimes when he does it I want to bop him on the head and yes, sometimes I have.

So here's the problem, we want to spend time with each other but when he tries to do it his way he messes it up. So what is the answer? I'm training him to sit and I'll come to him. If he will sit down, I will bend over, or get on my knees or do whatever it takes for us to be together, but in order for this to work, I have to come to him. If it isn't done this way, the moment is both spoiled and lost.

We do the same thing. We try to come to God on our terms and that won't work. We try to work our way to Him, pay our way to Him, try to guilt Him into being with us and none of these things work. God doesn't owe us the time of day let alone anything else, including life. But we keep trying to make ourselves right with Him and do it by our rules. It must break His heart to watch us struggle so trying to do something He's already done, open the way to Him. He watches us. We bat at the air, huff and puff and bull our way usually into situations that are worse than they were when we started. Why? Because we want to treat God like Burger King and "have it our way". You know, this I like, that I don't so I'll build my own "buffet religion".

It's been done. Jesus tells us in the Gospel of John, 14:6. "I am the Way, the Truth and the Life and no one comes to the Father except by Me." There, that's it. Price paid. Path made. Door open. The way to the Father is through the Son. It's that simple. But no, we go on trying to make it harder than God ever intended it to be. Question, why would God create us if He didn't intend to spend time with us? Did He want some cosmic toy to play with and then put away when He got bored? The answer is, of course not. Its obvious that God wants to spend time with His children, and that's us. Does that surprise you? It shouldn't.

So why are you trying to go to a Father that has already come to you and shown you the way to Him? It's done. Come to the Father by the blood of the Son. Don't wait. It's worth doing. It's worth doing now.

―――――――― ――――――――

IF I COULD HAVE JUST SPOKEN HIS LANGUAGE.

> "And the Word became flesh, and dwelt among us,
> and we saw His glory, glory as of the only begotten
> from the Father, full of grace and truth.
>
> **John 1:14 (New American Standard Bible)**

Biscuit is just about the best "cummear" dog I've ever had. For those of you who don't speak "suthurn", "cummear" is pronounced come here. But anyway, he is. I can remember before this though. When Biscuit first became a part of our family, I would call and whistle, call and whistle and call and whistle trying to get him to "cummear". It was usually at night and raining! There I was: barefoot, t-shirt, shorts, wet, and definitely not in a festive mood. Finally, finally, he would round the corner of the house and give me that "what" look. You know the one; total disrespect and what's your problem, written all over it. If he had only known that my standing out there and calling him was for his benefit, not mine. I wouldn't be any warmer or drier in the house if he were there. I wanted him to be warm and dry. As for me, I just wanted his companionship. It didn't matter to my comfort any more or any less if he listened to me and got warm and dry. I wanted him to be where he really needed to be--in the house, with the family, where we could all just be together.

I'll never forget the first time I called him and he came running. I whistled and called out his name and he came flying around the corner of the house in the back yard and I was thrilled. All I could think of was what could I give him? I could now lavish all the love, blessings, and affection on him that I wanted to. You see, I couldn't reward him for not coming to me. Yes, I still loved him when he didn't, but I couldn't reward bad behavior. But now. Now all I wanted to do was get him a treat, buy him a car, put him in my lap and scratch on him until he didn't want to be scratched anymore, which with Biscuit is never. He'll let you scratch him until you die of starvation sitting there and scratching.

But here was the problem. I didn't speak Biscuit language. I wanted to shower him with my love and spend time with him, but he didn't understand me. If I could have become a dog and spoken "dog-ese" to him it would have been so much simpler. Do you see where I'm going? God just wants to lavish His love on us and bless us and spend time with us. So what did He do? He became one of us, spoke our language and showed us how much He loved us.

Are you listening? He still speaks today in a language of love, wisdom, correction, direction. Just for us. So that He can spend time with us, hold us in His lap and scratch us until we feel so at home there that we can imagine being any place else. Come to Him today. You're missing a lot of love and blessings if you don't.

JUST SPENDING TIME TOGETHER.

"Come, let us bow down in worship, let us kneel before the LORD our Maker; for he is our God and we are the people of his pasture, the flock under his care."

Psalm 95:6-8 (New International Version)

Sometimes when I'm getting ready in the morning, Biscuit will come into the bathroom while I'm shaving and brushing my teeth and just lay on the rug in the bathroom at my feet. When he does this I do what any strong red blooded American macho man would, I talk baby talk to him. Actually I'll talk to him in a low voice, tell him how much I love him, reach down and scratch him and just spend a few minutes loving on him and being close to him. This usually ends when Catfish comes in like a freight train. Fortunately his collar does rattle all most as much as a railroad crossing bell so we know when he's coming (that's truly helpful at night when this is the last sound you hear before being jumped on in bed by a sixty pound goof of a puppy).

Anyhow, when Catfish gets there, the "soft" time is over, its now time for rough housing and insanity. Now don't get me wrong, I love Catfish very much, as much as Biscuit, but sometimes I just feel like "being". Know what I mean? At those times, with Biscuit, or for that matter Catfish, at my feet, I want to bless whoever is near me. It's so wonderful to have someone like Biscuit at my feet at these times and because of his desire to be near me, to be with me, to be at my feet, he's the one who gets blessed and gets my love lavished on him. Now for those of you who are saying, "what about his wife and daughter?" I love them more, this is just kind of different. It's a love of someone who will literally lay at my feet.

Sometimes God just wants to spend time with His children, love on them and bless them. Please allow me to give this human terms here. When

He so wants to lavish His love on someone and when there's someone who is already wanting to be so close to Him that they have taken time to spend time in worship of Him, who do you think is the first one to be blessed and to have His love lavished on them?

Have you spent time with God this way? Have you just come to Him, no agenda in mind, no problem for Him to fix, just to be in His presence? Too often the only time we spend with God is when we want to treat Him like Santa Claus, "give me this, or I need that". Just spend some unselfish time with Him today. If you will spend time at God's feet, you'll find it well worth your while.

LET THE GAMES BEGIN

"See, I have written your name on the palms of my hands."
Isaiah 49:16 (New Living Translation)

Let the games begin. Biscuit and Catfish play/fight almost constantly. Usually Catfish starts it by biting Biscuit or hitting him with his paw. After that, Biscuit is growling and chasing Catfish throughout the house and out of the door. Our door out of the kitchen goes onto a screened patio and into the back yard. You remember, the back yard, the one where Catfish dug the swimming pool for us? During pretty weather we will leave both the kitchen door and the patio door propped open so that the boys can roam throughout the house and into the back yard. The reason for this is the more they play during the day, the better they sleep at night and when you have two creatures like these, they can indeed keep you awake at night with their antics.

Most of the time both of the boys sleep with Ari. This is a funny sight to see. Picture this, one 70 pound and one 40 pound dog on a single, yes I said single bed with our beloved daughter. If I ever go into her room to wake her up its like looking at an opened can of sardines and too often smells the same. Don't jump to conclusions and don't get ahead of me. The smell usually comes from the dogs... Usually.

When Catfish and Biscuit come out of Ari's room in the morning they run, leap, fling themselves about and just generally go nuts with Elain and me telling us good morning and then they want to continue leaping and such if we will just open the back door and let the games begin. It's so much fun to watch them. Catfish is about twice as fast as Biscuit and can literally run circles around him. This frustrates Biscuit and makes him mad. Therefore, he is now mad at Catfish because Catfish won't let himself be caught and the process accelerates. The madder Biscuit gets, the less Catfish wants to be caught because by now Biscuit sole purpose in life is to bring injury to Catfish. Like I said, its fun to watch in a "boy that's sick" sort of way. Catfish flying around the back yard, Biscuit giving chase, barking and trying to cut Catfish off at the pass.

That's how the sleeping and waking arrangements usually are. Sometimes however, Ari is out of town so the boys sleep with Elain and me. What's amazing is that these two can have ample room in Ari's single bed yet they don't have enough room in a king sized bed. They want to snuggle with each other yet both find it necessary to touch both Elain and me at the same time. Catfish's favorite spot with us is under my armpit in a ball. Biscuit on the other hand would prefer for me to sleep on my back and he wriggles his way between my legs so that I'm sleeping as bow-legged as if I were catching a nap while riding my horse with the herd. As you can well imagine, these are not the most comfortable sleeping arrangements there are.

Sometimes, on rare occasions Elain gets up before I do in the morning. Ok, I'm lying, she always gets up before I do in the morning. But when she does, the boys will follow her and want to go outside again...and again, and again and again. When they come back in, they want to play what we lovingly refer to as "plop on pop" a game involving them treating me and the bed like a cross between a wrestling arena and a trampoline. Loads of fun. They leap about and play while I do what any good father would do. I pretend I'm asleep and hope that they'll go away and bother Elain wherever she is. (What a loving husband).

So here's the picture. Biscuit and Catfish growling, running jumping all over the bed and me. And then there's my part, lying perfectly still, playing dead and hoping beyond hope that those two run out of the room and I'll catch a few more minutes of snooze time. I know, what a great parent also.

Here's what I want to point out to you. With all of my imperfections I still am very much in love with Elain, Ari, Biscuit and Catfish. Not paying attention all of the time. Pretending to be asleep when I'm not. Not getting up to let them out when I'm really awake so that Elain will do it. Oh yeah, I forgot to mention that. But even with all of these short comings, I love them all dearly. With every fiber of my being, with every beat of my heart, an imperfect person loving with all he possibly can.

Our Heavenly Father IS however perfect. He doesn't sleep. He doesn't even pretend to sleep. He's always awake and always has us both on His mind and on His heart. Why else would He send His Son to pay our sin debt if He didn't care about us deeply? There are times in our lives, in my life, where I forget this. I look at the circumstances around me and think that God has forgotten about me and where I am. So what should I do? What should we do at those times? It's not always easy, but we should remember those times when we really felt close to God and realize that He is just as close when times are hard as He was when life felt better. He hasn't abandoned us. He hasn't forgotten about us. No matter what has happened, He is still madly and passionately in love with us. And it is such a deep love even to the point of self-sacrifice and death.

When you're feeling lonely, remember, you're not. Not only does your Father still love you, He never stopped. He has left His people on this planet to encourage one another. Not a church building, but people. If you need a church home, find one where the people truly love. If you are in a church, how well are you showing the love that God has entrusted you with? Be what you were designed to be, authentic people who never pretend to be loving and caring.

LET'S LIVE IN DADDY'S LAP

> "No, in all these things we are more than conquerors through him who loved us. For I am convinced that neither death nor life, neither angels nor demons, neither the present nor the future, nor any powers, neither height nor depth, nor anything else in all creation, will be able to separate us from the love of God that is in Christ Jesus our Lord."
>
> Romans 8:37-39 (New International Version)

Biscuit and Catfish have a new game they play. It's called "Let's both try to fit in Dad's lap at the same time." Sound fun? It is for them. Not so much for me. Here's how they play it. Biscuit will jump up into my lap for me to scratch him. He loves to be scratched. He will even grab your hand with his paw to put it where he wants to be scratched: head, chest, stomach. Sometimes he leans backwards for you to hold him on his back leaning against my chest and arm for me to scratch him on his stomach and chest in something we call playing Teddy bear. So far cute, right? Enter Catfish. Now what some of you know and some don't is that Biscuit weighs about thirty three pounds. Catfish, on the other hand, weighs about sixty plus pounds. All of the sudden, here comes the leap. Catfish has entered the picture. First he wants to lick you for about ten minutes with his tongue the size of a shovel. Remember the Muhammad-Ali, George Foreman fight years ago? Ali did a thing called "rope-a-dope". It kept Foreman from hitting him in the face and head while wearing out the bigger stronger man in the process. This is what I have to do with Catfish. I "rope-a-dope" while he's trying to wash my face until he moves on to something else.

By this time, Biscuit has had enough of Catfish and jumps out of my lap, growling at Catfish and the situation. Jealousy abounds. Then Catfish decides to try to curl up in my lap. One of Catfish's nicknames is "Tea cup Catahoula". Not only does he think that he's Biscuit's size, he actually thinks that he is smaller as evidenced by the fact that Biscuit always beats him up. Neither one of them knows that Catfish is bigger. Got the picture now? I have sixty plus pounds of writhing goof ball in my lap, because Catfish is never not writhing. And he thinks that he is small enough to roll around and be treated like Biscuit. No problem though, Catfish never stays any place for more than a few minutes. Almost immediately he is standing up, "tromping" all over me and leaping off of me and the chair in order to see what other confusion and destruction he can cause.

Does this sound like a complete "pain" to you? Well let me tell you something, I love it. When those two want to jump up into my lap, love on me and get loved by me its just the greatest. Right this moment Catfish is trying to get in my lap, in my office, in a chair that is most assuredly not big enough for two. I think he wants to help me type but that's a bit of a problem, he has no thumbs. Again, I love it.

Our Heavenly Father is the same way. He wants us in His lap. Does He have a lap like a human being has a lap? I don't know. But I do know that He wants us in His presence and close by twenty four hours a day, seven days a week, the closer the better.

So then, why don't we do it? Is it because we feel that we have done something and He wouldn't want to be in our presence? Let me put that to rest, yes we have. Wait. Before you run away, let me explain. His relationship with us isn't based on our goodness, but rather on His. He wants to be with us because HE wants to be with us. He wants to be the closer the better because HE wants to be the closer the better. He loves, not loved, but loves us so much that nothing can stand between us and Him unless we let it be there. No sin, no attitude, no past, no present, no future can separate us from the love of God.

Why aren't you, why aren't we closer to Him? His lap is waiting. His arms are waiting. His heart is waiting. He has even said to all of us, "Come to me all of you who are weary and heavy laden and I will give you rest". (Matt 11:28) But it doesn't stop there. He will give us rest, love, wisdom, peace all that we could ever possibly need. Just crawl into His lap. He loves it when His children do that. He doesn't care how much you weigh or how many burdens you are carrying around with you that add to the weight. He is willing and able to take them from you and give you rest. Go. Now. Don't hesitate. He's there. He loves you. He eagerly waits for you. Scoot along.

I CAN'T SCRATCH THEM BOTH AT THE SAME TIME, MY ARMS AREN'T LONG ENOUGH.

"Rejoice with those who rejoice, and weep with those who weep."
Romans 12:15 (New American Standard Bible)

Biscuit and Catfish have reached the point that they both want attention at the same time. Catfish doesn't care what else I'm doing, as long as one hand is on him and he's getting scratched. Biscuit, on the other hand, wants complete undivided attention when his Majesty wants it. If I'm scratching him and Catfish comes along, Biscuit will "mumph" and wander off. Now here is the picture. Biscuit is sitting beside me, standing on the floor, curled around my head, wherever he happens to be and here comes Catfish. You need to really see this picture. Have you ever seen movies with dinosaurs in them. Remember the Tyrannosaurus Rex? You know, the one with big back legs, real small front legs and a head the size of a freight train full of teeth? That's what it looks like when Catfish is coming to break up the spa massage Biscuit expects. All of the sudden, Catfish, giant head and all, is coming at you at ramming speed. I hear "ker-flop, ker-flop, ker-flop, as feet the size of hams hit the floor. You can hear the wind whistling between his ears since there's nothing to stop the flow of the breeze and he crashes into Biscuit and me. Now Catfish doesn't mind that Biscuit is getting scratched, actually, with Catfish it's half scratch him, half he eats my hand, but as I said before, Biscuit gets bent out of shape. So he will walk out of reach and pout. Here's the problem. My arms aren't long enough to scratch them both. If Biscuit walks away, I can't reach both he and Catfish at the same time. I so wish that Biscuit would realize that just because I scratch Catfish, it doesn't mean that I can't scratch him and love on him at the same time.

Fortunately for us, God's arms are long. He can, and does, love on all of us at the same time. Regardless if we are in America, China, or wherever, He can be there where we are and is always able and available to show us His love if we will just let Him. Why are you walking away and "mumphing" like Biscuit does when God loves on someone else? Don't you know that His love for you hasn't diminished in the least just because He wants to bless others? He wants all of His children to be blessed. Be joyful that He blesses others also. He still loves you just as much and fortunately, His arms are long enough to scratch all of us at the same time.

SOMETIMES LIFE IS A BATTERING RAM

"Finally, brethren, whatever is true, whatever is honorable, whatever is right, whatever is pure, whatever is lovely, whatever is of good repute, if there is any excellence and if anything worthy of praise, dwell on these things."
Philippians 4:8 (New American Standard Bible)

Biscuit mostly tolerates Catfish. Don't get me wrong, he cares for him, loves him like the rest of us do, but mostly, he just tolerates him. Catfish is a little brother and you know what is thought of little brothers by big brothers. They're a pain. No difference here. From time to time Biscuit wants to spend time with me. Just him and me. He wants me to scratch on him, love on him and play with him. One of those moments when one-on-one is what is wanted and needed.

What usually happens is when this starts, Catfish's "hey they're doing something without me" radar goes into effect and he "comes a running". There we are, Biscuit and me, just being us and along comes this head about the size of a freight train attached to about a million pounds of mutt barging in. Needless to say, the one-on-one deep communication is over. Now the battle begins. Both want one on one, but it's like this. Biscuit still wants one on one with me so he's mad at Catfish. Catfish wants one on one with me and one on one with Biscuit, which is mathematically impossible. I want one on one with both of them, feel the impossibility growing? And as you can well imagine, the free for all ensues. The quiet time is over, the riot barges in.

This happens in our lives also. Have you ever been driving someplace, music blaring and then realize that you have to find some place on some street? What do you do? You turn down the radio, CD player, whatever is making the noise. Why? Looking for something is not auditory, it's visual.

However, you don't need that distraction barging in right then. You need one on one with your eyes so that you can focus on the task at hand.

We need one on one time with God. Time to just be in His presence, for whatever reason--to praise, to laugh, to cry, to petition, but time to just "be" with Him. And then life barges in. With it comes tugs, pulls, misdirections, and sometimes just noise. How can we shut it out? How can we focus on what both we and our Heavenly Father wants? I wish I had a simple answer for this but I don't. There's no "three steps to" or "how to's" to help, it's just a chore. There are so many things that compete for our time and our minds that it is a continuous battle to have our minds staid on the things that are right.

What we have to do is this, make time for being alone with God, make a place to be alone with God. You don't have to build Solomon's temple in your back yard or apartment. Your place can be your bedroom, a corner of the family room, kitchen table or your office. Even outside under a tree would be good. As far as time is concerned I know what you're saying, " I don't have time for that". Right? Then why is it we have time for television, magazines and other things? Listen to this, we make time for what is important. If television is more important than time with the Creator of the Universe, then that's what you'll do. But I'll guarantee you this, time spent with the One who gave His Son's life for you is better than someone who's telling you to live for today and forget about tomorrow. Logical?

What's holding you back? Don't know what to say? Start off with His Words to you. Start off with telling Him about the cares that weigh deeply on your heart. He doesn't care what you say. He just wants you to start. Now when you do, the cares of this world will come battering in like Catfish does when he wants attention and it will take multiple times for you to be able to set them aside, but set them aside. They'll still be there when you get through. As I have matured in my walk with God I have found more and more comfort, conformation, direction, encouragement and so many other helpful things have happened in my time with Him. I have no magic you don't have. The "magic" is that an all powerful God will meet us there, wherever "there" is. Go there today. He's waiting.

———————— ————————

THE DAY I FOUND OUT BISCUIT WASN'T PERFECT

"Or do you not know that your body is a temple of the Holy Spirit who is in you, whom you have from God, and that you are not your own? "For you have been bought with a price: therefore glorify God in your body."

1 Corinthians 6:19-20 (New American Standard Bible)

You know, there are those in your life that you think can do no wrong. They always say the right thing, wear the right clothes, they're always at the right place at the right time with the right people. Carly Simon wrote in a song years, although it seems like yesterday, ago, "you're so vain, you prob'ly think this song is about you." That kind of person. The James Bondian, Cary Grant, Hootie and the Blowfish kind of guy. Ok, I just threw the last one in to see if you were awake. But you know the person I'm talking about. With a look of fake forlornness I say to you, Biscuit was that person to me.

When he was young he came into our lives from "Animal Adoption Day" at Petsmart. Don't ever go there on Saturday's unless it is your intention to come home with a new pet. Yes, he quickly won and warmed our hearts on that cold January, February, no, I was right the first time. Yes, that wintry day in December our lives were changed forever by a little guy who was part terrier, part all kinds of other dogs and part spider monkey, his legs reach from here to there. He became an immediate much loved part of the family.

Ari didn't mind sleeping on the floor so Biscuit could have a bed. After all, he had been homeless and abandoned, a child of the streets. That he didn't wind up in a gang, boosting cars, shoplifting and stealing purses is just by the grace of God and the dog catcher.

We treated him well. We got special food just for him. As a matter of fact it was even called "dog food". Special toys. Ari didn't mind giving up her video games. He looked like he had fun with them. With no thumbs he couldn't press the buttons but he could watch the screen and bark. We gave him all any dog, dare I say it, any child could ask for.

In the beginning all was well. Only once when he came home from the orphanage did he have an "accident" on the floor. Do you ever wonder why they call them accidents? It's like whatever was in them jumps out and they had nothing to do with it. But anyhow. Only one accident. Biscuit is the best "come here" dog I've ever been around. He almost immediately knew to come when his beloved father called. He slept with Elain and me. He went where we went. He ate where we are, which is hard on the knees sometimes.

One of our favorite things to do was this. Biscuit is mainly a back yard dog. Fenced in, big enough to run and play in, good bushes to hide behind and play chase, but every now and then we would make a trip to the front yard. On some days when I needed to get the garbage cans or the mail, Biscuit would go with me. Another thing he loved to do was when one of us got home he would run out of the door to meet us. A joyous reunion. Quite often these things were done at night because that's when we all would finally get home. Running through the front yard, playing chase, running into one another's arms. Good times. Good times. And then that day.

There was nothing special about that day. The sun shone, birds sang, ducks ducked. Just an ordinary day. Both Ari, my little darling daughter, and I got home early, me before her. When she drove up I said those magic words to Biscuit that he loved to hear, "Sister's home", which in doggy talk means run to the door, throw yourself against and see if you can knock it off of its hinges or scratch through it. As he ran out to greet Ari I realized that another person had a schedule different that day than others, the mail man, postman, letter carrier, the bane and demon of every dog ever to set foot on Terra Ferma.

Biscuit was out the door like a shot. I never knew that he could run so fast as he did that day. Across the carport, out the driveway, across the street, into the neighbor's yard and up to the mail man. As Ari yelled to the public servant, "just stand still, he doesn't bite," the unthinkable happened--Biscuit bit him. Yes, you heard me right. My beloved son. Heart of my heart, love of my life, bit the postman. A sad day!

After some serious talking, begging, promising that he had never done this before and never do so again, the postman relented and didn't cook and eat him. It was however close. But now there was a problem. Biscuit had done a bad thing. Not just a bad thing, a very bad thing. He wasn't my perfect little guy any more. His front yard privileges had to be permanently revoked, even to just running out of the door and getting in the car to go someplace. I could no longer take the chance of this crime being repeated. Not to mention that he didn't look both ways when crossing the street which could have been fatal. No, now there was a chink in the armor, and flaw in the relationship and fly in the buttermilk (shoo fly shoo). Things were and quite frankly are, different.

I love him every bit as much as I ever did, but we can't do things as we did because of choices he made. We've made choices that have hurt our relationship with our Heavenly Father also, haven't we? Choices made at a young age, perhaps teenage years or even recently that cause our walk with Him to not be where it once was. Here's the difference. I didn't know that Biscuit was going to run and bite. God knew that you and I were going to mess up. Before time began He knew. Ask me how. I don't know, but He did. Before we even thought about the deed or the consequences He knew and prepared a way for forgiveness and also a way to mend our relationship. It cost Him a great deal. It cost Him His Son. But we need to know that this was the price, the only price and the only way for us to be in His presence, for His Son to "redeem" us, to pay that price for our sin and rebellion. I know that those are words we don't like to use about perfect us, maybe other, but not us, but folks, that's just the way it is. We're not perfect. Since Adam, we never have been, and on this planet, never will be. But in God's eyes, in God's heart, once you've recognized Jesus for Who He is, we're perfect to the Creator and Sustainer of the Universe.

I love Biscuit, but a price had to be paid. That price was no more front yard privileges. God loves us but a price had to be paid and that was Jesus being sacrificed on the Cross for us. Steep sin, steep price. God believes. . .no, God knows that you're worth it. So start living like you are. "Paid in full." Great words!

THE SAME PRICE IS PAID FOR ALL

"For Christ also died for sins once for all, the just for the unjust, so that He might bring us to God, having been put to death in the flesh, but made alive in the spirit;"
1 Peter 3:18 (New American Standard Bible)

Neither Biscuit nor Catfish come from the most exclusive of bloodlines. As a matter of fact, we got both of them from a pet shelter. We had lost our Dalmatian Bueller, named after Ferris Bueller, after almost fourteen years and sorely missed his companionship and his love. After a while, we decided to adopt another family member and along came Biscuit. A word to the wise, if you have a heart that is any softer than concrete don't ever go to an animal shelter or any place where they have pet adoptions. We saw Biscuit, Biscuit saw us, boom we were hooked. I still have the hook marks in my lip where he reeled me in. Don't ever think you pick them, they pick you. One of the things that the people do who work at the shelters really gets you hooked. They let you hold the puppies. You can walk around with them in your arms. They'll even go outside with you and let you play with them there. Then my friend, you just TRY to put them back in their cage. He named himself by immediately running into our back yard when we got him home and devouring all of the biscuits Elain had thrown back there for the birds. They still haven't forgiven him. Now he's the spoiled rotten child of Elain and Michael, ruler of the house and heir to all he surveys.

Next came Catfish, the Big Slurp, Shovel Tongue, Elvis (he does one lip up thing), the Vicious Fish. Let me give you some advice. Never let your daughter go get dog food when the pet adoption people are at the pet store. This was the phone call, "Daddy, I've found the cutest LITTLE Catahoula Cur puppy to be Biscuit's brother." What word stood out in that sentence? That's right, LITTLE. Sixty five pounds later he still thinks he's the Teacup Cur and can fit in our shirt pocket. He can almost fold himself up to where he can.

Here's a problem. Biscuit thinks that he is better than Catfish. Catfish is a dog, Biscuit is a person with no thumbs. Biscuit has forgotten that the same shelter we got Catfish from we got him from. He thinks he's better now. He's forgotten that we had to pay the same price for him that we did for Catfish. Some Christians forget that Jesus had to pay the same price for them as he did for the "bad" people. Me and crack head, same price.

I am a diabetic. The new testing instrument manufacturers try to sell me on the fact that I don't need as much blood for my blood tests now. The amount of blood is not the problem. Piercing my skin several times a day is the problem. No matter whether it is a drop of blood or a half of a drop—it hurts! No matter how good you are, Jesus had to be pierced. I may not be as bad as the next guy, but the same price had to be paid for me too. (Reread scripture above.) Quit looking down on that other person. They are no better nor any worse. Not worth less nor more than we are. We caused Jesus to have to go to the Cross just as much as any person who ever lived or will ever live. Do this right now--thank Our Heavenly Father for paying the price for you. This isn't between you and the next guy, me and the next guy. It's between you and God and me and God. Never think that we let Jesus "off easy" because we're so good. If we're so good, then why did He have to come and be pierced? Think about it.

THERE'S A TRAIN WRECK IN OUR HOUSE

"The thief comes only to steal and kill and destroy; I came that they may have life, and have it abundantly."

John 10:10 (New American Standard Bible)

Yes, you read that right. There is a train wreck in our house. Not the kind you think. We don't have locomotives and diesel engines running in our back yard, although I think that would be very cool. What we do have is Catfish. He can run through the house and cause disaster where no disaster existed before. He weighs between 65 and 70 pounds, has a head the size of a T-Rex and will "bust" in on anyone and anything going on in the household that he is not a part of that particular instant. For example, try to pay attention to anyone other than him. Scratch Biscuit, read a book, breathe or dare I say it, hug my bride, and there he comes. Panting like a locomotive, full head of steam, bearing down on you with no brakes..... train wreck. Walls shake, people and things go to the floor, Catfish gets into trouble and Biscuit points and laughs because it's not him. Train wrecks. Twenty four hours a day, seven days a week, train wrecks. We've all had them. We all have them. No life, no person is exempt. The problem is that most of our train wrecks aren't cute like playing with Catfish and Biscuit. Real train wrecks are painful and scary.

Most train wrecks in life are surprising and potentially disastrous. In life we all experience train wrecks: we're going to have to cut back and you.... we've looked at your x-rays and we've found...I've met someone else and... I'm calling about the past due payment. . . You know what I mean, train wrecks that we didn't see coming. Train wrecks that we maybe couldn't even have avoided if we had known about them. Collisions that knock us off our feet, onto our backs and sometimes we don't know if we'll ever be the same again after them. Pain, suffering, permanent change (usually not for the better), out of nowhere. Train wrecks.

Sometimes they' re funny. Like Catfish running into Elain, Ari, Biscuit, me. Most of the time they aren't. They're just what they sound like, train wrecks. That sound as your life crashes in around you. Your fault, someone else's fault, no ones's fault. The results are still the same. Broken hearts, broken bodies, broken bank accounts, all painful, all disastrous. Bad? Yes. Hopeless? No. There is One who no matter what the train wreck, is able to not only right the train, but get it back on track and pull it, push it, do whatever it takes to get that wrecked life moving again.

I'm writing this story Easter week, a time when all of time and all of humanity had a cosmic train wreck. Where you may say? At the Cross. That's where man and God met to pay the price for all of the wrong, all of the sin that ever was and ever will be. All the train wrecks. All the crashes of life that make us believe that sometimes death would be preferable. Think about Jesus. Think about this week. He entered Jerusalem with people clamoring for him and calling out His name. His followers ready to take over Jerusalem, next stop, Rome. By the end of the week He was hanging from a Roman Cross, the worst of the worst, not just capital punishment, but the most evil Rome could muster. Being punished for what some considered a petty crime worthy only of a beating if that much. Now think about this, Jesus saw this train wreck coming. Not only did He know about it minutes ahead, hours ahead, days ahead, He know about it before time began.

Question: what would you do if you saw a train wreck coming and it looked like you might be a part of it? I'll tell you what I would do. I would run, screaming like a little girl. Jesus didn't. He asked His Father, Our Father, for strength. Not to run out of the way, but to stand firm and absorb the full fury of something far greater than a train wreck, the wrath of God on a humanity that didn't deserve forgiveness, but rather incineration. He stood. Square shouldered, firm, jaw set, eyes ahead ready to take that which was rushing toward Him. And it was not preceded by a train whistle warning, but rather the quiet kiss of a friend. Have your train wrecks been preceded by the kiss of a friend? Many of mine have.

So what do we do? After the wreck and our eyes finally open, we see the devastation around us. Bodies, hopes, dreams all seemingly wrecked beyond repair. Not a pretty sight? Neither was Golgotha, the Place of the Skull, the place where Jesus was crucified. Think about this. Even Jesus didn't leave that train wreck on that day alive. Wow! Therefore, He knows what it like to not only be in a train wreck, but to get killed in one.

So what did He do? He let the Father have His way. God didn't want Jesus dead. He wanted Him alive. Therefore Jesus had life. God doesn't want us dead in this world either. He wants us alive. I'm not saying that we are never going to die. Unless Jesus comes back beforehand, we all will die. What I'm saying is John 10:10 (See verse above). Abundant life! We can have an abundant life not only after a train wreck but even during a train wreck.

Look around you. What you or I sometimes consider a train wreck may not be but gentle rain to others. But even if its huge, what are you going to do, let it defeat you or are you going to remember that we have a Brother in Jesus Who experienced train wrecks more than once and a Father Who not only will see us through the train wreck but also has the power to help us survive and go on again. Maybe not the same way we went before, it may just be another way. But I promise you this, He won't give up on you and if the King of the Universe won't give up on you, why should you give up on you?

WHEN WE'RE BAD, WHY DO WE WANT TO RUN FROM THE ONE WHO FORGIVES US?

> But the LORD God called to the man, "Where are you?" He answered, "I heard you in the garden, and I was afraid because I was naked; so I hid."
>
> **Genesis 3:9-11 (New International Version)**

The other day, Biscuit did what he doesn't do as often as he used to, but still does too often. He believes that it is part of his job description to scare the mailperson as they are pushing the mail through the mail slot, and to attack the mail scattering it throughout the house. We have discussed this in multiple family meetings but the lesson still seems to not have stuck.

I came home recently and found mail in every room of the house, he had done an excellent job of both distributing and destroying all that had come through the mail slot. (I wish I could teach him to do that with the junk mail only, but we're still working on that.) Anyway, he knows when he's done wrong, all I have to do is pick up a piece of the mail. I don't need a dirty look, raised voice, or even raised eyebrow. He just knows. When I did pick up the dismembered mail he headed for the door.

It made me think of how we all are with God. Had Biscuit done wrong? Yes. Were there going to be consequences for his actions? Yes. Was I mad at him? Yes? But going to quit loving him? Of course not. Another question that his reaction brought to my mind was, "where was he going to hide?" In the back yard? My backyard? How could he hide there? That was mine also.

Do you see the ridiculousness of the situation? We can't hide from God. He not only knows who we are and how we are going to act, but also knows where we are, because wherever we are, He's there also. When

God called out to Adam in the garden, He knew where Adam was, he was giving Adam the opportunity to come to Him instead of running from Him.

Why is it when we do wrong we run from the very One who wants to and will forgive us if we will truly go to Him and ask forgiveness with a repentant heart? Is that what you are doing? Is that where you are today? Why? Do you think what you've done too bad? Impossible. Is the person you feel you are too dirty? Same word, impossible. God loves you. God wants to forgive you. Let Him. Go to Him with a heart that truly wants to be forgiven and changed and He will do exactly that.

--- ---

WHY CAN'T THEY DRINK WATER LIKE ANYONE ELSE?

"He who believes in Me, as the Scripture said, 'From his innermost being will flow rivers of living water.'"

John 7:38 (New American Standard Bible)

I taught Biscuit how to do something some time ago that I thought was cute. Now I realize that I am more trained in the doing of this than he is. One day, while brushing my teeth he jumped with his front paws on the counter in the bathroom. He seemed to be fascinated with the water running out of the faucet and in to the sink. Having seen this before, I was not so enthralled as he, but never the less I watched him as he watched the water. As you may be able to tell from this story, I am easily entertained. After a while I asked Biscuit if wanted some water. He said, "yes father, I truly would, for I am thirsty". I did too hear him say that. I took a plastic cup from the stack, filled it with water and he gingerly drank from it, not spilling a drop or lapping on my hand in a "doggish" manner. This became a regular event when I was in the bathroom. Biscuit would come in, sit and stare at the running water and when I was finished I would give him a cup or two, whatever he wanted. Cute, huh? Enter Catfish.

Yes, the crazy son. Killer of stuffed animals, cushions from sofas and often, sofas themselves. It didn't matter what Biscuit and I were doing, if Catfish wasn't doing it also, he soon would be with all the finesse of a tornado. Whirling, leaping, chewing. barking just wanting to be a part of the activity, whatever the activity was. This time it was to learn how to drink from an eight ounce cup of water. Seventy pound dog, eight ounce cup of water. See the problem?

This is how it went. First, Catfish would watch Biscuit drink from the cup for a few, a very few, seconds and then decide enough time has passed, time for me to drink. When I would stop him from that he decided to bite Biscuit on the leg until his attention was away from the cup of water and then Catfish would take over. He treated the cup and the water as if he had to have it, and have it now, that there would be no more water and he would have lost out on getting his.

After much discussion and pulling back by the collar Catfish eventually learned that I was not going to neglect him, nor was the water going to run out. He would sit somewhat patiently and wait on his turn. After Biscuit drank one cup, Catfish was ready. I then had to train him to wait for Biscuit to drink his fill then I would turn my attention to him. It took a while, but he learned.

Now a bigger problem. Remember the seventy pound/eight ounce ratio problem we discussed earlier? Add to this the T-Rex head, the train wreck, Captain Destructo. In comes Catfish to drink his fill. Head way too big for that cup. Tongue able to slurp more out of the cup than in to the mouth and what do we have? Water, lots of water, lots and lots of water. On the floor, my hand, my arm my legs. Please remember, I have to hold the cup by the bottom for both of them and bend at the waist to place the cup in a position that is comfortable for them to drink, and Lord knows, it has to be comfortable for them. So Catfish is slurping, chugging and drenching himself, me and the entire bathroom. I wouldn't change it for the world.

Here's what happens now. Either one or both will sit in the hallway outside of the bathroom as if to tell me that its time for me to serve his majesties their fresh water. The other day while doing this I was thinking, "you know what would be a good idea? If we got a bowl, a big bowl, filled it with water, and put it someplace where they could get to it at their convenience and then, yes maybe then, I wouldn't have to do this". Then, in my infinite wisdom I answered myself. I says to myself, I says, "Self, you've already done that. There is a bowl, a big bowl filled with water in a convenient place where these two can drink till their little heart's content. I'm just the nitwit that still does this regardless of what is in place already to take care of their wants and needs in this area."

Why am I telling you this? First off, I thought it was funny. Secondly to let you know how we sometimes think like this. As Biscuit was first fascinated by the running water, we are fascinated by the fact that there is running Living Water that is there to quench us from the dryness of the world and its promises of happiness and peace that are like mirages in the desert. We also feel like Catfish in that if someone else is being blessed then the blessings will dry up and we won't get ours. This is where the realization that the water was never going to run out for Biscuit and Catfish and they didn't have to compete for it. It would always be there. And finally, the expectation that I know that if I ask, and if I ask what my Father has promised to give me, He will provide. If I will meet Him in the place where He wants me to meet Him, He will be there. Ready, willing, able to provide for the thirst that I have with Water that will never run out.

What makes you thirsty today? Have you gone to the Well for water that will not run out or are you trying to do it yourself. Think about this, if you could take care of your own thirst and quench it forever, you already would have. Right? Go today. Go where thirst can be quenched. Go where the One Who quenches your thirst is. Go to Jesus.

ALONG CAME ANOTHER...

Blueberry, also known as Blue, Baby Blue, Zombie Dog, and the ever popular Paper Cut with Lemon Juice, was added to the pack in July, 2006. You would think going to a Red, White & Blueberry Festival (which now you know why she was named Blueberry) in a small town would not result in coming home with another four-footed furry child, but we have the knack. There she was, the LAST ONE of her litter being given away, sitting in a cardboard box with a red ribbon around her neck, how could we not bring her home! Once getting her home with her big brothers, Biscuit and Catfish, we realized Blue was a little on the skittish side and as she's grown that skittishness gives her the appearance of being downright schizo at times which we try to nicely say as being "twitchy". But we love her anyway and we consider her our "special child", which means it takes a little more patience in loving her and living with her. But that's okay, because I'm certain God looks at a lot of us that same way!!

Blue is a mix of Australian Shepherd and Border Collie and has become the Alpha Female of the pack (which means she can beat up on Catfish and Highway, but more about that later).

―――――――― ――――――――

….. AND THEN, THERE WAS BLUEBERRY

"But I have this against you, that you have left your first love."
Revelation 2:4 (New American Standard Bible)

You know how there are some people in your life that when spoken of, it comes across as, "oh yeah, and then there's so and so"? That's kind of how it is with Blueberry. I love her. I love her. I love her. But she has the personality of a paper cut… with lemon juice.

Blue came to us from the Red, White and Blueberry Festival in Clinton, Louisiana, one fourth of July. As Elain, Ari and I walked up to the festivities, we saw the sign that makes children jump for joy and father's cringe, FREE PUPPIES. All of the sudden, I realized that I was walking alone, and Elain and Ari had "bee-lined for the Free Puppy Pavilion. Well folks, Blue was the *last one*. Oh, and you have to say that with a cry in your voice, as if you were writing a country song.

It didn't take us but a short while to find out that Blue was "skittish". That's a nice way to say "flakey". She growled at everyone and everything. Wouldn't come when you called, you'd have thought she was a cat, very aloof and just overall, kind of nil on the personality front. But she's mine and I love her.

Blue reminds me a lot of a mean Christian. Did you know that there are mean Christians out there? They were mean lost people, and now they're mean Christians. Impossible you say? Wrong. Please remember that salvation and sanctification are two different things. Salvation is instantaneous. "I accept what Jesus did for me on the Cross and recognize him as my Savior." It's that quick. Sanctification is the rest of your life. It's learning how to be more Christ like in this world. It seems that some people have accepted Jesus as Savior, but not as Lord. Salvation? Yes, Change my personality? No. Therefore, mean Christians, Christians with a bad attitude, Christians you'd rather not be around. But still nevertheless, Christians, <u>saved</u> by God, owned by God, loved by God.

Blue, after four years, is coming around. She will play with us, come to us, snuggle with us. She still has her quirks. Any of the other pups get in her space, you'd think they were trying to kidnap her and sell her to the Egyptians, but she's coming around.

How about you? Are you coming around or did you stop at salvation? Do people enjoy being around you or do they run when they see you coming? You know, there are a lot of people who would be a Christian, except that they met one. Does your attitude and personality enhance the Kingdom of Heaven or detract from it? Is Jesus your Lord, or just your Savior? If He's Lord, we bow our knee to Him and live for Him. Now tell me, how can you live for Jesus and not seek to be Christ like?

It's your choice and if Blue, the papercut with lemon juice can start making the better choices, certainly you can too.

BLUBERRY DOESN'T THINK THERE ARE ENOUGH BLESSINGS TO GO AROUND

"For this reason I say to you, do not be worried about your life, as to what you will eat or what you will drink; nor for your body, as to what you will put on. Is not life more than food, and the body more than clothing? Look at the birds of the air, that they do not sow, nor reap nor gather into barns, and yet your heavenly Father feeds them. Are you not worth much more than they?"
Matthew 6:25-27 (New American Standard Bible)

Blueberry is coming around. It's only taken three years, but she's starting to act like a loving pup rather than a zombie. In the past, when either Elain or I, or other dogs would try to get in her space, she would get stiff-legged, arch her back and start circling like a shark. Quite often, she still does that, but with a smile on her face, it's baby steps.

Now, she'll play with me. She really likes, I won't say loves, to jump up on our bed and have me pick and push on her. She'll roll around and just play like normal dogs do, as long as it's just me and her. If any other of the herd comes in, jumps up on the bed, walks through the room, looks at her, or breathes, the back is arched, legs go stiff and the growl of death emanates from her lips. We go from "fun time" to "I'm going to kill somebody" in an instant. When, all along, we could have continued indefinitely, it is a king sized bed. But noooo, Blue becomes an "all for me, none for anybody else" being in the blink of an eye.

I even try to continue playing. I hug her. I push and play, but once someone else is breathing her air, it's all over but the temper tantrum. She doesn't realize that we can continue to spend time, and have fun together, even though there are others in the room.

I know what some of you are thinking, "What a dumb dog?" Yep, but remember what I said, she's come a long way. But let me tell you, don't get too superior in your thoughts about Blue, we do the same thing. How, you say? Glad you asked.

How many times have you heard of, or seen God bless someone, and your first thought was, "if he deserves that, then I should deserve two of them". Jealousy, the Green-eyed Monster. Too many times we show deep empathy for the neighbor whose home catches on fire, but just don't let them build back one better than ours. We look at our neighbor's new car and instead of reveling in their good fortune, we feel that they should never have a car better than ours. Sound familiar?

Unlike me and you, God's arms aren't short. He has blessings for everyone, attention for everyone, love for everyone, all at the same time. If God blesses you, He still has enough to bless others. If He blesses others, you're still fine. He isn't going to run out, not today, tomorrow, or any day.

Remember, God not only owns the cattle on a thousand hills, He owns the hills also. Don't worry about others, their good fortune, or the wonderful things that happen to them. First, that's just wrong. What they have or don't have is none of your business. Remember, if you spend too much time tending someone else's garden, yours will die. But also remember, God has ample of Himself for all of us.

Dip into that well, it's deep and never ending.

———————— ————————

BLUE DIDN'T WANT TO BE BRUSHED

"All that the Father gives Me will come to Me, and the one who comes to Me I will certainly not cast out."

John 6:37 (New American Standard Bible)

A few week-ends ago, it was "bath time". Not mine, I bathe every week even if I don't need it. It was bath time for the Mutton Heads, the Thundering Herd, the Fearsome Foursome. Getting mentally, emotionally and physically ready for this is akin to training camp in the NFL. You stretch, put on the right clothing, get the equipment ready, set your mind right, put on your game face, and go at it.

When we're ready, and it does take both Elain and I, we first seek volunteers. Volunteers are a rarity at this time, treat time yes, bath time no. So then begins the baby talk. Sometimes this fools one of them, too often I'm sure they think, "I've heard that siren's song before and it got me soaked, not again, oh loving parents." So then we have to begin the tirade. "Biscuit, Catfish, Blue, Highway, GET OVER HERE." This is followed by one of us ultimately having to go get one of them. Now the fun can begin. Whichever one gets the honor of being the initial sacrifice to the water god looks at us the entire time as if screaming, "It buuuurrrrns!" We all know that it doesn't, but perception is reality.

Upon finishing the first one's bath, he or she is let loose without drying him/her off. That means that the clean puppy shakes off and then romps through the yard because he/she has been scrubbed, rubbed on, baby talked to and now, cooled off on a usually blistering hot day. The routine is repeated four times until all, us included, are soaked to the bone, but feeling so much better about ourselves. We're all on the patio, running through the yard, wind in our hair (or fur) and a feeling of accomplishment.

One of the things that happen after all four are finished is the ritual of brushing. All of them know the brush. All of them love the brush. There's usually no calling twice for someone to come get brushed. There's usually a non-ending circular line of brush addicts awaiting their turn until your arm wears out or falls off. They quite often, push each other out of the way, head butt Elain or I to get our attention again and just generally make a wonderful nuisance of themselves.

The other day during that family time, a strange thing happened. As everyone jockeyed and rejockeyed for position, Blue didn't want to participate in the brushing ritual. I brushed everyone, then brushed everyone again and noticed I hadn't brushed her. I called her over, but she wouldn't come. I was confused. I reminded her that this wasn't something that she liked, but something that she loved. I told her how much I loved her and how much I really wanted to expend myself for her. "I'll brush you. You just have to stand there and be brushed", I told her. Still nothing. No matter what I did, how much I coaxed, how much I reached for her, she wouldn't come get something that she really wanted and needed. There are times we get enough fur off of them to knit a whole new puppy. But Blue wouldn't come. How I wish that I could make her understand what she was missing out on and how much I wanted to do this for her, still, no brushing.

It makes me think of how much God has always wanted to do for us, but too often we don't come to him. We don't know why many times, but we still don't come. I can only speak for me here, but I wonder, is it hard headedness, guilt, occupied with other things, too much of the world going on right now? I don't know. I just know that it happens to all of us.

So God did something better. He made Himself one of us and then came to us. He looked like us, dressed like us, spoke a language that we understood, told stories that we could understand, and the whole time prepared us to be ready to spend more time with Him. I wish I could have done that with Blue, spoken her language and let her know that this was for her, but I couldn't. Thank You God that You could and You did.

If you're wondering if Blue ever got brushed, yep. About an hour later, after I had taken a shower, gotten cleaned up and was in the wonderful, climate controlled home, she came, stood in front of me like they all do when it is brushing time and basically told me, "now is a good time for a brushing". What did I do? With right on my side, the moment passed and totally occupied with something else, I got up, went outside, got the brush and had a few moments of quality time with my little contrary one. But, that's what daddies do.

HIGHWAY, ONCE WAS LOST, BUT NOW SHE'S FOUND

Highway, also known as Princess Sac-a-Mud, Tank, Battering Ram Head, Little Baby Girl, became a part of the pack and our family in Spring, 2007 and we weren't anywhere near a PetsMart or a festival at the time. Elain was returning from grocery shopping and as she pulled onto Hwy. 68 in the rural area we live in, in the distance she saw a creature darting back and forth across the highway. Was it a little deer, or a rodent of unusual size, she could not tell, but she pulled off of the highway onto the grass shoulder and the creature followed her car to the side of the road. Peering over the front fender of the car, Elain realized it was indeed a dog straining its neck to see Elain in the car. Elain's nurturing instinct took over more than her fear and she opened the passenger car door. As she did, the dog dropped to its belly and crawled up to the side of the car whining. Elain extended her hand and the dog came further and put her head in Elain's hand. Elain called me and asked, "what am I going to do". I told her she could either put the dog in her car and bring her home, or never have a good night's sleep again, there did not seem to be any other option. So, Elain gingerly helps the little waif into the car

and continued down the road to our house at which point the orphan puts her head in Elain's lap at first and then looks up and grins a big toothy grin. It was at that moment Elain realized, "I've got a Pit Bull in my lap!!" and that's how we got Highway and she got her name.

And yes, she is indeed a Bull Terrier of the Staffordshire line and while some may still wrongly label her as a Pit Bull, she's our baby girl with an unbelievably sweet demeanor that belies the ferocious behavior resulting in the atrocities committed upon these breeds. Ask Highway, she still carries the scars from whoever she had to live with before we found her. Amazing Grace. . . aren't we glad we all have access to it!

HIGHWAY GIVES PIT BULLS A BAD NAME

"But an hour is coming, and now is, when the true worshipers will worship the Father in spirit and truth; for such people the Father seeks to be His worshipers. "God is spirit, and those who worship Him must worship in spirit and truth."

John 4:23-24 (New American Standard)

Recently, a friend was over visiting. As she sat on the sofa and we visited, there of course, was a dog in her lap. Some sofas have throw pillows, ours has lap dogs. After about thirty minutes of Highway, her name tells you where we found her, our friend asked, "What kind of dog is Highway?" I answered, a Pit Bull." She jumped up, "I'm afraid of Pit Bulls." I looked at her dumbfounded. "It's the same dog that you've had in your lap for thirty minutes. She hasn't changed." Our friend, who is a dear friend, an educated person had it built up in her mind that these were bad animals, and that was that. What I need you to understand about Highway is she gives Pit Bulls a bad name. She cuddles, whines, runs from the other dogs and is scared to death of any noise this side of a humming bird's wing. I do feel remiss if I don't add a little something here about the bad rap that Pit Bulls get. A Pit Bull is a dog, no more, no less. I'm old enough to remember when German Shepherds were the bad dogs, then Doberman's, then Chow's, then Rotweiler's. Now, it's the Pit Bulls turn. Next week, month, year, we'll choose another.

Preconceived notions, we all have them. This is good. This is bad. Why? I don't know. It's just always been that way. This isn't just in our day to day preferences concerning clothes to wear, movies we see, or foods we eat. Brussel Sprouts aren't bad just because I don't like them. There are hundreds of other reasons. Do you know why most churches fight and have splits? It isn't over theological differences. It isn't over the pastor falling or "investing" the offering in his choice for the winner of the Kentucky Derby. It's over the most mundane, every day stuff that you can think of. The color of the choir robes, what type of carpet in the worship center (Doesn't that turn your stomach, arguing over furniture in the WORSHIP CENTER). One of the biggest fights in churches is what type of music to play. Let me set this to rest for you. God likes all types of music. I love the argument, "I don't like this new music. I like the old stuff." My response to that is, " What old stuff? Miriam's song, "The Horse and Rider Are Thrown Into the Sea?" That's old stuff. The Psalms? That's old stuff. These songs that were written 100-150 years ago, they're practically contemporary. What you meant to say was, "I like what I like. I like my kind of music." Guess what? That's ok. It's ok for you to like the music you like and PREFER that this style be played. But, guess what else? It's equally, yes equally, ok for others to like a different style of music and prefer it to be played. There's a very old saying with this line of thinking. How do you tell good music from bad music? Simple, I like good music. I don't like bad music. The conundrum is, who gets to decide? For the record, it ALL belongs to Him. Satan hasn't taken some forms of music and claimed them as his own. We've led ourselves to believe he has, but either God is in control, or He isn't. He is much less interested in the style of music or the instruments used than the heart that's singing it. Is the worship true? That's what counts.

Just as our friend's preconceived notion that all pit bulls are bad, she pushed Highway away and in so doing, lost the fellowship she was having with a very sweet cuddly puppy that only had good intentions. Maybe, just maybe, we all need to expand our preferences based on what we actually know about a person or choice or situation instead of what we think we know. It just might make our fellowship sweeter and our worship full of spirit and truth.

HIGHWAY IS THE VELCRO PUPPY

"The Lord is not slow about His promise, as some count slowness, but is patient toward you, not wishing for any to perish but for all to come to repentance."

2 Peter 3:9 (New American Standard Bible)

Do you have different names for the same dogs? You know what I mean, you've named your dog whatever, but, with their actions, they keep giving themselves new names, ours do. Biscuit is Roly Poly, he could say the same of me. Catfish is Dinosaur Head. Blueberry is The Twitchy One, and one of Highway's many names is Velcro Puppy.

She has another one also that I'll tell you about first, it's her Native American name, Princess Sac-a-mud. You have to understand, Highway weighs somewhere between 70 and 400 pounds. She is one of the most solid creatures I've ever seen in my life. When she wants to be someplace, it usually happens. Quite often, we'll hear a thump as she head butts a door to get in. It usually works, even on doors that open the opposite directions, she's going in. "Thump", then the door swings open with the same decorum of a SWAT team's entrance. And then, Highway is amongst us. Now it's kind of important that you know this because of the rest of the story.

One of her other names, as I've already said, is Velcro Puppy. She likes to snuggle with Elain, with me, with whoever is visiting with us, she just likes to snuggle. It's always cute, but sometimes, shall we say, it's cumbersome, especially in the bed.

If she is able to wheedle her way into bed with Elain and me, she's great about not jumping around when we're trying to sleep, but she'll attach herself to my left side from ankle to chest, snuggling up to me to the point that it's like having a wall on that side of me. Remember the Sac-a mud nickname? Picture her on my left, her head against my foot. I'm unable to roll to my left, move my left leg, left arm, and if I turn my head to my left, did I mention that her head was at my feet? Princess Sac-a –mud has made her presence know….in a large way.

I can pretty much forget comfortable sleep until I muster the strength, yes and desire to get her OUT OF THE ROOM. I lay there, weigh the advantages of her being gone, think about how much I could use the sleep, and then whine to myself that I REALLY don't want to move. Been there?

It is truly a pain. Guess what? I love it. How can I not love someone who wants to snuggle, to cuddle, to be that close to me? But sometimes, I don't have the stamina or the patience to allow it to go on.

Isn't it wonderful that God isn't human? If we want to snuggle, to cuddle, to be in His presence, He says "sure, come on". Night or day, good times or bad, days that are too long or nights that are too long, "come on". He is never too tired, too busy, too occupied with others to push us aside.

When was the last time you spent some quality time with Him? Just you and God, one on one, telling Him who much you love Him, and Him letting you cuddle up and forget about the day, it's problems, your short comings and the trials that await outside the door?

Now would be a good time. Go ahead. Put the book down. I don't mind. I'd much rather you listen to His words than mine. It doesn't matter if it is a.m. or p.m., raining or sunny, if you've done right or done wrong, He's right there, right now waiting to snuggle with you.

THE FEARSOME FOURSOME – WHERE DID WE GO WRONG??!!

Four dogs, living in the house, that's four feet times four which equals 16 feet that must be wiped off when there's rainy weather, that's a 25 pound bag of dog food (along with sprinkles now) a week, that's pandemonium at bath time and enough fur balls to knit who knows how many other puppies! But, in the chaos, we have more love than anyone deserves and we wouldn't want it any other way!!

BISCUIT IS A FUN NAZI

"Taste and see that the LORD is good; How blessed is the man who takes refuge in Him!

Psalm 34:8 (New American Standard Bible)

That's right, you read correctly. Biscuit, the Number 1 Son, the king of all he surveys, the local deity, is a fun Nazi. Oh, it's ok if he's the one having the fun. If he's running, leaping and celebrating his supreme place in the family, all is cool. But let others laugh, jump, run in circles and just have a good time in general and his ire is raised.

I see it happen all of the time. If Catfish, Blue and Highway start playing with each other, especially if we're outside having fun, Biscuit starts barking as if to say, "enough of this frivolity, let's get serious". Why, I don't know, because he likes to have fun too. I guess fun has to be on his terms. It's funny to watch. We're all playing and Biscuit is standing there like a long faced drill instructor, griping about the lightness of the moment. And, as obviously happens with all members of the master race, his belly starts itching and he has to scratch it. Get this picture in your head, we're playing, he's barking and scratching his belly like the two are connected.

Does it remind you of anything? All churches, all organizations have a fun Nazi. He or she is the person that can't stand for others to be happy. In church, they're the ones who let you know, and very quickly, that this is no place for smiling, laughter or any light-heartedness. This is a place for guilt, shame and to continually remember what a worm you are and how much God wants to punish you for everything you've ever done. As a matter of fact, the only time this person wants to see smiles in church, is when the pastor recognized from the pulpit what a wonderful person the fun Nazi is, and how the covered dish dinner would have exploded without their divine intervention, or their uncompromising efforts to make sure that the parking lot is never used by outsiders or lost neighborhood people.

Nobody needs them. But everybody has them. Fun Nazis are about as much good as their name implies. So, why do we have so many of them? Because that's how they were raised. They, perhaps, were taught that God is sitting in Heaven holding a quiver full to the brim with lightning bolts, just waiting on us to do something wrong so He can turn us to toast. Where's the logic there? Does it stand to reason that a God Who gave us everything that we have, the very air that we breathe, and even His Only Begotten Son to pay the price for our sin would then tell us that we aren't to enjoy the very things He gave us, that's just ridiculous and again, completely illogical.

So then, why do we live that way? Conditioning. We've self-taught ourselves to believe that a loving God is too good to be true. Guess what? He isn't. Read of His love. Experience His forgiveness. Taste, and see that He is good. When you're in His will and having a good time of it, He has a good time too. Isn't that what loving Fathers do? Why not pass that along to the fun Nazi in your life?

FROM BLESSING, TO RIGHT, TO DEMAND

"Then He said to them, Beware, and be on your guard against every form of greed; for not even when one has an abundance does his life consist of his possessions."

Luke 12:15 (New American Standard Bible)

Supper time with four walking, living breathing food vacuums is interesting. No joke, they look at each others bowl like we're going to give one solid gold and the other dirt. They whine and gripe like they've never eaten before, and this might be the last chance. Highway, Pit Bull, has to be fed separately because she eats bowl and all in one ravenous gulp. Biscuit and Catfish kind of stand around to see what's going to happen. And Blue, the "skittish" one, runs around to all bowls. It has nothing to do with eating, she just wants to give everyone grief. Now, as much fun as this sounds like, we haven't gotten to the part that really makes us think, "where did we go wrong?"

Because Biscuit is older now, we started adding to his dry dog food, (don't tell him it's dog food), some softer, shredded looking food. We started calling it "sprinkles". I don't know why, we just did. After a while, we could put the regular food in his bowl and he would sit and wait for his sprinkles. Well, as they do, when playing musical food dishes, the others stumbled upon the sprinkles. Soon, all were addicted to sprinkles and Elain and I now had to add yet another step to the already crazy supper routine. Who says you can't teach an old dog to do new tricks? Elain and I learned how to do this in no time.

Now, on top of the food, everyone wants sprinkles. Even Highway, who eats food, bowl and flooring expects them now. I don't even know how she ever even saw the sprinkles since she eats in a different room from the rest. They look at the food in their bowls and stare at us with distain. It's like their eyes speak as if we've forgotten to put their napkins in their laps at a five star restaurant. What once was a special privilege has now moved to a right, and yes, even a demand. They now expect this of us and we have not done right by them if we don't do this daily.

We can be the same way with God. We think that our definition of blessings should be changed to "every days". We want from God. We want from God now. And we want what we want and nothing else, any other way will do. Let me give you a good working definition of a blessing. Inhale--no really--do it. Inhale, now exhale. The guarantee just ran out. The next breath is a blessing. God doesn't owe us the next breath. He blesses us with the next breath. Anything above and beyond that is blessing on blessing.

Please understand. I'm not picking on you. I'm the same way you are. The vast majority of us are the same way. We just forget and have to be reminded. I had a seminary professor who used to say, "You knew that. You just forgot that you knew that." We do this all of the time. We forget that every day things are truly blessings to us.

When the four "mutton heads" come bugging us at dinner time, it hilarious to watch. The anticipation in their faces is priceless. If you are a dog lover, then you know what I'm about to say is truth. If you aren't a dog lover and you say that this is bologna, then why are you reading this book? Dogs understand a lot of what their people say to them. The Thundering Herd starts bugging us at about 5:30 p.m. each afternoon. Elain or I, usually Elain says, "who wants some good supper?" The ritual begins and chaos ensues. We love watching them. We love the fact that they jump on our laps to get our attention. We love just about every part of it.

What they, and we too often forget is this, everything that they have, everything that they eat, the very bowl that they're eating out of, is mine. None of it is theirs. They owe it all to me. Not ugly, just fact. None of what we have is really ours. It all belongs to God, and as a blessing, He lets us have it, use it, keep it. It's blessing on blessing.

Today, how are you treating the blessings that God has given you to watch, to tend, to love and have for Him? If you haven't realized it or taken the time, you might want to start today thanking Him instead of demanding of Him. As a hymn of old says, "When upon life's billows you are tempest-tossed, When you are discouraged, thinking all is lost, Count your many blessings, name them one by one, And it will surprise you what the Lord hath done." (**Count your Blessings,** Words by Johnson Oatman Jr, 1897)

GOD KNOWS MORE THAN WE DO

"For I know the plans that I have for you, declares the LORD, plans for welfare and not for calamity to give you a future and a hope."

Jeremiah 29:11 (New American Standard Bible)

For those of you who don't know, the Fearsome Foursome are "in the house" pets. They go outside to take care of business, to run, romp, play, bark at leaves and each other, but most of the rest of the time, they are inside the house. Catfish is the funniest one about this. We'll all go sit on the patio, and after a while I'll hear someone scratching the patio door behind me. My first thought is, who did I leave in the house?" Then I realize, it's Catfish scratching to get IN the house. It's like he says, "enough of the outside, it's hot, I'm going in." After staring at him for a few minutes I realize, he's the smart one. I'm sitting in the heat; he wants to go into the air conditioning.

But one thing they all try to do is this. When Elain and I go out the front door to go for a walk in the evenings, they charge the door like there's magic puppy food on the other side and want to get out with us. Please understand, we have a nice sized house and it sits on about a one acre, fenced lot. They have a ton of room to commune with nature, but like any of us, it's where they can't go that intrigues and entices them. The siren's call of the front yard and all that lies beyond is more than they think they can stand.

What they don't realize and we do, they really don't know of the danger in that part of the world. Out front are streets, cars, no fences, people who don't care, savage squirrels and a rogue bird or two. Once you get out there, I don't have enough of me to chase you down and save you from yourself. You will be left to your own devices and the consequences of your choices and actions.

Didn't Adam and Eve do the same thing? God said, "Stay within the parameters of the Garden. Leave the one tree in the middle alone, it's Mine, and everything will be fine." What did they do? They went straight for the forbidden and had to suffer the consequences.

Now as we sit here with our spiritual 20/20 hindsight, we say what idiots they were and how they really messed it up for the rest of us. But we still do the same things today. "Oh no, I haven't messed up anything for humanity. I'm not like those others." Really? How about gossip, back biting, that shady deduction on your Income Taxes, coveting what your neighbor has, on and on and on. Did you know that many of these sins are listed in the Bible right next to murder and adultery? Ouch!

Why do you think God tells us not to do these things? Simple, He's smarter than us. He knows the things that will harm us long before we do. As a matter of fact, he knew what was good and bad for us before we were born.

When you have a tax question, you go to a tax expert. When you have a legal question, a legal expert. But when we have a moral, spiritual, right or wrong question, we want to go to the popular magazine of the day, or let the Hollywood celebrity who's been married and divorced five times and can't make up their minds if we came from fish or were discovered by aliens. That's who we look to for direction and model ourselves after. And why? If they were so happy, why so many divorces? Do happy people really fall in and out of "love" four times in one year?

Why not go to Someone who gave us the "how to" manual two thousand years ago, and the rules for right and wrong which haven't changed? Let's truly go to Someone who is smarter than us. I tell people all of the time that I'm not a smart man, so I've done the next best thing, I married up and surround myself with smart people.

Surround yourself with smart people, beginning with the Smartest, the One Who Wrote the Book.

HOW THE HECK DID WE GET FOUR?

"You did not choose me, but I chose you and appointed you to go and bear fruit—fruit that will last."

John 15:16 (New International Version)

We have four dogs. I don't know why we have four dogs. We didn't set out to have four dogs. I don't believe there was some cosmic design for us to have four dogs. But we have four dogs. We have Biscuit, Catfish, Blueberry, and Highway, four, count them, four dogs.

I honestly sit and look at them sometimes and ask myself, "How did we get so many? "This wasn't the idea." They tear about the house. Tear up the house. Make and have smells that aren't the most pleasant. At times they distract Elain and me from things that we really need to do right then, LIKE WRITE THIS STORY. They cost money for food, vet bills, toys, replacing furniture and clothing. As a matter of fact, they truly don't add a great deal to anything here, except for one thing: we love them, we have chosen to have companionship with them and shower as much love on them as we possibly can.

Each one of them was chosen by us. We looked at them among other dogs or all by themselves, or in dire straits and said, "I'll take you. Come with me". Sometimes we took them to be ours in spite of who they were. Highway is a Pit Bull, not the most sought after dog for a family dog, but we picked her, she's ours. They can be smelly, rotten smelly sometimes. They don't add anything to the whole, they don't make the world a better place to live, yet they're ours, we love them, end of controversy.

Did you know that God feels the same for us? We haven't tricked Him into loving us, although many of us try. We don't add anything to what He already has, He has it all. We couldn't buy our way into His favor. He just chose us, in spite of our short comings, in spite of our sin, in spite of the fact that we add nothing to that which is already complete, and in spite of our smelliness sometimes, He chose us.

If you go all the way back to the people of Israel when God chose them in the Bible, He didn't do so because of any specialness about them, except for the fact that He chose to do so. They weren't a great people. As a matter of fact, quite often, when another country was in a bad mood, they beat up Israel. Nevertheless, they were chosen by God.

"Chosen by God", doesn't that have a good sound to it? "Chosen by God". Remember in grade school or junior high when you might have been the last one chosen for the game? Didn't feel too good, did it? At first, I was that guy, not too big, not too fast, not too popular, but eventually I was chosen. It was normally after my younger sister, but I did get chosen. However, as time went on, I got bigger, faster and a little more popular, so I started getting chosen sooner, and some times, even first.

Guess what? God doesn't care. Fastest/slowest, largest/smallest, most popular/totally unpopular, God chooses you. Why? Because He wants too. It's called grace. He chooses us because He chooses us. We don't add anything. He doesn't owe us anything. We don't bring anything to the table, He just chooses us.

As I look at this thundering herd of mutts, in all honesty, I do think of where they'd be without our choosing. It really doesn't matter though, you know why, because we DID choose them. Today, if someone or something tried to get to them, or get at them, whoever it was, whatever it was, it would have to go through Elain and me to do so. Why, because we've chosen them, that's why. They are ours. Whatever we have to do to protect, direct or discipline, that's what we'll do, just because they're ours.

If you're feeling all alone today, don't be, because you aren't. If you're reading this book, this story, it's because you're either are a Christian, or you're searching for answers. If either of those is the case, then know that there is One Who has chosen you and merely waits for you to answer His call. Smelly, rotten smelly, it doesn't matter, He's chosen you. In the midst of it all, you can certainly feel good about that.

SOMETIMES FOUR IS TOO MANY

"But You, O Lord, are a God full of compassion, and gracious, longsuffering and abundant in mercy and truth."

Psalm 86:15 (New King James Version)

I did not know we had a pack until the Dog Whisperer informed me through his TV program, but we do—a thundering herd of dogs. Sometimes I feel like I have more four footed creatures around me than Romulus and Remus did, and they were raised by wolves.

First, and he would say foremost, there's Biscuit. He is the Alpha male, local deity, whatever you want to call him as long as it has to do with Numero Uno. He's the smallest of the bunch, but nobody knows it. He's rules the roost with an iron paw. His slightest wish is carried out immediately and with fervor. Secondly, Catfish, seventy pounds of Catahoula Cur. As I've said before, he's why you don't let your daughter go to the pet store on pet adoption day. She'll call you and talk about the "cutest little puppy". And you'll let her bring him home. But Catfish has about the best personality of any living creature I've ever been around. He's just happy to be. Next, there's Blueberry, she was the last in the give away box, and I'll be honest, I didn't know that this would traumatize her so. She's neurotic sometimes, well to be honest, all the time. Finally, Highway and her name says how we got her. Could you leave any creature on the side of the road that crawls up to your car on her belly and cries? Neither could we and now there are four!

All of them I love. All of them are permanently in my heart. Quite frankly, I wish I had four hands so I could pet all of them at once. Let me tell you, I've tried and they've expected me to do so. The problem arises in that, there's only one of me. They clamor for my attention. Isn't it amazing with dogs, if you're gone for ten minutes or ten hours it's like you just got home from the war. They whine. They shove each other out of the way. Catfish and Highway are best at this. We sometimes call Catfish, dinosaur head, because it's so big. But, there's still only one of me. No matter how much I want to spread myself. And too be honest, some days, how much I don't want to spread myself, there's still just the one. No human can be expected to be "on" twenty four hours a day, seven days a week. It's just impossible. No matter how much we love. No matter how much we want to love, we have our limits.

Please, don't think that I'm waning in my affection for my puppies, I'm not. I still love them with all of me. I just "run out of me" from time to time. They can be the most loving pains you've ever seen.

I surely am glad God isn't that way. We. . .let's just make it personal--I, clamor for His attention. I whine when I don't get it. If I could, I'd push people out of the way who seem to be closer than me. I want, I want, I want. And what does He do? He keeps right on loving me. There is enough of Him to go around. Remember what I said about wishing that I had more hands? I don't know if God has hands or not. That's a word called anthropomorphism, giving human qualities to God. We really don't know if He has hands, feet, eyes. He's bigger than me and some day, I'll see for myself.

Back to the main thought, God does have enough of him to go around. He is omnipresent, every where. He is omniscient, all knowing. He never sleeps. At 3:00 a.m. when I need Him, there He is. And because of Jesus, He'll never turn His face away from me.

Like I said, I love my pups, but sometimes four is four too many. Isn't it amazing that, for God, multiple billions aren't too many? He has ongoing love for all, ongoing patience for all, enough of Him for all. Don't get me wrong, this doesn't mean that we won't suffer consequences for our actions, but He will never throw up His hands and say, "enough of you, get away from me".

Amazing. . .grace.

Other Stories That Have Struck My Fancy

————————  ————————

Obviously, these stories are not about the Fearsome Foursome. They are just thoughts I have had over the years about things that can make you say, hmmm. . . so I've added a few for your enjoyment. Enjoy!!

CHECK YOUR ASSETS, YOUR ATTITUDE AND YOUR LUGGAGE.

In my home state, Louisiana, we have a name for something added as a little extra prize or gift, it is called Lagniappe, (pronounced lan-yap). This is really not so much a story as my observations as a pastor over the years. However, whether you are a pastor of a church, entering a new employment situation or a new relationship, I think you'll find some helpful insights in the following pages. I hope you enjoy my Lagniappe to you.-- RME

I. Check your Assets.

What does your church do well? What do they have a natural affinity for? Do you have good singers? Then use music to reach the pews and the community. Are there several good, strong witness-minded men? (Several, you say? Yeah, right). Whatever the number, then use them. Anyone who wants to play, let them play, there is no maximum or minimum number on the team. At our church, the saints here are very strong in fellowship. Therefore, we do many activities in the community which both lost and saved can be invited to for a wonderful time. What do I mean? Special musicals. Music is what I call "non-threatening evangelism". Everyone likes music. Christmas musicals, Easter musicals, 4th of July musicals, our people love them all and when someone in the pew or the community sees someone enjoying their time in church, they might want to be a part of that too.

II. Check your Attitude.

Checking attitudes does not only include that of the pastor, which will be discussed in checking your luggage, but also that of his immediate family, as well as the church family.

Question One. Is your family in this with you? If not, why not? How is *your* attitude with your family? Do they feel like they're number 11 on a list of 10? When my family and I were in evangelism and singing, traveling to many churches, we used to, and here is a bad word, JUDGE a pastor by his wife. If she was friendly and nice, we felt that he was also. If she was standoffish and unfriendly, we knew that he was faking it. Because if he was the same way with her and his family that he was with us, then why didn't his wife want to be around at ministry time?

Question Two. What is the attitude of your church? Entirely too many pastor's sole determination concerning changing churches is based on money issues. How big is the package? If a bi-vocational pastor, then moving to a fully funded ministry will be the driver. If fully funded, the driver may be that you're presently at $40,000 and the new church is offering $50,000 and on and on and on. However, a key point that desperately needs to be taken into consideration when contemplating a change is, does the philosophy of ministry of the perspective church line up with yours? Are you extremely evangelistic and they are "us four, no more or holy fortress" in their thinking? It is my solemn belief that churches want one of two things: revival or cemetery maintenance. If the latter is what they want, that is their prerogative, you just need to know this fact before you go there. "Yes, but I can change them." I'm not arguing, I'm just saying know what you're walking into before the door has to hit you on the backside because you envisioned the church going in one direction and the congregation wasn't with you. Oh, and about changing churches, never run from a church. It's ok to run to one, but not from one. If you've done your homework on the church in question, you greatly increase the possibility of being "on the same page" with that church. When interviewing with a church, I say that the first interview is theirs, the second is mine. Meaning, the first time we talk you start deciding if you want me to be there, the second conversation is me interviewing them to see if this is someplace that I feel God is leading me to be.

III. Check your Luggage.

If it seems that I've put the bulk of the article under the heading of the pastor's responsibility, I have. Sorry guys. You are the ones who said that you were called into the ministry. No one ever said it would be easy.

Too many pastors today think that wherever they are is just a stopover or stepping stone to the bigger and better church. They never unpack their spiritual, emotional, or even sometimes, physical luggage. Their focus is always on the new horizon ahead. That perfect church that is going to meet all their needs, where they can preach the Gospel, grow the church from 500 to 5000, change the world and get out of this back wadi in Nowheresville. Question, did you know that the church where you are can feel that? They know. They can tell that you're treating them like they're junior high football and you should be in the NFL.

Maybe, just maybe, God loves them as much as He loves you and He thinks that they deserve some good preaching and pastoring for a long time. The average "tenure" of a pastor these days is approximately 18 months. We pastors cry about "church bosses" whose attitude is "I was here before you came, I'll be here after you're gone." Problem is, it's true. If we're only looking to stay here until we can make it to Broadway, they <u>will</u> be here after we are gone, and for some pastors who never fully let themselves be here in the first place, they're here right now and we aren't.

Let yourself go. You've heard it, "grow where you're planted." People ask us often "why are you at a small church?" Answer, "because that's where God has us." Don't you think that He knows where you are? He knows your address and He knows when its time to change it.

Remember Matthew 25:21 "His master replied, 'Well done, good and faithful servant! You have been faithful with a few things; I will put you in charge of many things. Come and share your master's happiness!' But let me ask you this, "what is 'a few things'?" Are those in front of you any less important to God than those at the mega-church? You may have the next Billy Graham in front of you. From where I sit, that's pretty big and adds up to "many things". Throw your heart, your everything into where you are and throw away that luggage too. This is God's church, and He might just grow it while you're there and wouldn't that be great?

--- ---

CRAZY 8s

"Consider the lilies, how they grow: they neither toil nor spin; but I tell you, not even Solomon in all his glory clothed himself like one of these."

Luke 12:27 (New American Standard Bible)

I remember a card game popular when I was a kid. Yes, I know, a kid is a baby goat and no longer a politically correct term to use, but, quite frankly, sometimes my friends and I had a great deal in common with baby goats: hard heads, eat anything, and the smell!!! But that's not why I'm writing this story. The card game I'm referring to was called Crazy 8s. I don't know if it's still around today or not, but this is how it worked: you tried to play off of your opponent's card, which was laying face up on the table, with a card of the same suit or the same number; 8s were wild and if you got a 2, you had to put a flower pot on your head or something like that. It was all pretty confusing. Quite often my mind would get really mixed up, and I would play a card that was kind of like a card on the table, because I had a card kind of like that in my hand. As I tried to think deeper and deeper, I got confuseder and confuseder (not really a word, but you know the feeling).

Life is like that, also. The more we try to figure it out, the more confused we get. Here's the deal. DON'T! You heard me right. Don't try to figure life out. You'll end up spending a lot of time awake when you should have been asleep, and you'll end up with less hair than you started with. I don't mean that we shouldn't prepare for tomorrow, just that we shouldn't fret over it.

God did not intend for us to be able to figure out our lives from beginning to end all at one time. He unfolds life before us in the same way He unfolds Himself before us. The people of the Old Testament learned the names of God because of events He unfolded before them; and when

He did, they realized that He was there to supply that need in their lives, too.

What needs do you have in your life today that you are fretting over? If your fretting fixes things, please send me your phone number--I've got some things I would like you to fret over for me. Let God be God in your life. Quit trying to run ahead of Him. Quit trying to do His job. Quit trying to be Him. Let God unfold His wonderful plans before your eyes, and you will be amazed at the plans for good and not for evil that He has for you (Jeremiah 20:11). Let's quit expecting God to give us a snake (Matthew 7:9-11) and realize that just as we want what is best for our children, God wants and has the best in mind for us. After all, what makes us, as sinful people, think we can ever be a better parent than our Heavenly Father?

Let's quit trying to figure it all out and control everything around us and realize that God is God and we aren't (Matthew 6:28-29).

SOMETIMES YOU JUST NEED TO DANCE IN THE HALL

"I am my beloved's and my beloved is mine,"
Song of Solomon 6:3 (New American Standard Bible)

One morning some time ago, we were getting ready to do battle with the day ahead. You know the kind of day I'm talking about. My bride was kind of "weepy," and I was not exactly the "spiritual giant" I needed to be for the day (yes, pastors get that way, too). Anyway, as we moped around the house, looking for the second sock that matched the one I already had on and looking at the bleak instead of the bright, a song that my wife and I really liked came on the CD we were playing. It's kind of a slow tune with words and lyrics that really mean a great deal to us. My heart went to those words, that song, and what it meant to us, and I kind of "slid" up beside my bride and said, "Let's dance." Right then, right there, we just slow danced in the hall. Tears came. Not just tears of "feeling low," but also tears of "I love you," "You mean so much to me," and "I would rather be here with you on a bleak day than anywhere else on a good day." We just held on to each other, swayed back and forth, and let the concerns take their correct and lower-valued place in the day.

I don't know what's going on in your world. Life may be perfect; but if you're like the rest of us, it's probably not. Let me offer you a suggestion. Walk up to your wife, tap her on the shoulder, and ask her to dance. You will be amazed, if she doesn't faint, at what that will do to your relationship with one another. Sometimes you need to cajole. Sometimes you need to discuss. But sometimes, you just need to dance in the hall.

DO WE WANT GOD TO BE SHALLOW HAL?

"The eye is the lamp of your body; when your eye is clear, your whole body also is full of light; but when it is bad, your body also is full of darkness."

Luke 11:34 (New American Standard Bible)

If you've seen the movie Shallow Hal, you know what it's about. For those who haven't, it's the story of a guy who is conditioned to not see the outer beauty of people but rather see what is in them, their inner beauty instead. He falls for a "larger" girl and goes through the movie seeing her as the most beautiful woman he has ever seen. At a point in the movie, his "eyes are opened" and he sees just her outer beauty, rejects her, and then realizes that indeed he has fallen in love with a girl who is so beautiful on the inside that her outer beauty is inconsequential. Ain't that sweet?

Isn't God that way? He doesn't just see our "outsides". He sees our inner beauty also, and quite frankly, that is much more important to Him than the color of our eyes, or thick luxurious hair. Now before you say, "isn't that great," and throw away the mirror, let me ask this question. "Do you really want God to see what's inside of you? Is your inner self--your spirit person, ready to be examined by God?" Ouch! I don't know if I want God to see what's in my heart and in my mind sometimes.

Guess whose fault that is? Not God's for "prying", but mine for calling myself His, but not continuously living like I am a child of His and a joint heir with Jesus. Question is, am I living my life as if God, or anybody for that matter, would be embarrassed by what they see in me?" Once again, OUCH!

How are you living your life? Your life is a legacy to your children and all who know you. What are you leaving to them, a life that is filled with things that you would rather NOT have them know, or more importantly, repeat in their lifestyles, or are you living a life that promotes those qualities that improve life, both here on good old planet Earth, and for eternity? Remember, especially parents, what we do in moderation, our children do "over the top". What do I mean? If you have your Playboy, you've taught them that pornography is ok. If you get drunk, you've told them that drug abuse is alright. If you treat you spouse disrespectfully, you've told them that spousal abuse is ok. If you tell them that they don't need to go to church, you've told them that God is unnecessary.

If your life isn't ready to stand up to the light, CHANGE IT. Now wasn't that simple? How do you do that? You start with a real, life changing relationship with God through His son Jesus. That is the only place that lasting change, from the inside out, will take place. Next, you find a church that preaches Him so that you, your family, your loved ones, will grown closer to God and to one another.

What are you waiting for? Isn't it about time that you moved from darkness to light? Is your life really the way you want it to be? Are you ready for God to see what's on the inside?

GOD FORGIVES, MOTORCYCLES DON'T

"Be anxious for nothing, but in everything by prayer and supplication with thanksgiving let your requests be made known to God."

Philippians 4:6 (New American Standard Bible)

As I write this to you, my 35 year dream sits in the motorcycle repair shop. That's right, the bike I have wanted since I was a small boy, one that rumbles, I put in a ditch the first day I brought it home. The saying goes, "stupid hurts". Well, that's the truth. I've got the sling for my shoulder and the pain pills to testify to that.

Another saying for us bikers, and I am still a biker, just a grounded one, is, "where you look is where you go." I'll explain. When riding a motorcycle, unless you are stopped or riding very slowly, you don't actually steer by turning the handle bars. The saying is Slow, Look, Lean and Roll. Slow down, look where you want to go, lean that way, and roll the accelerator up.

As I turned out of my driveway I was ready for the sun on my face and the wind in my hair. Since I was wearing a full-face helmet both of the above didn't really happen, but the rumble of the bike was music to my ears and caused my heart to beat in anticipation of what my "first", did you get that number? FIRST, spin around the block was going to be like. At the stop sign I waited for a car that was about 2 miles away to get by so as to not have any, I mean any, safety problems putting a damper on the maiden voyage of Easy Rider Ellerbe.

I turned left, accelerated, and that's when I noticed the ditch that I had passed a few hundred times before, but never really noticed. "Boy, that puppy's really deep", I thought as I LOOKED at the ditch now in front of me. I was mesmerized. I mean totally hypnotized. And guess what? What I looked at, I went to. Just like I stated earlier, what I focused on, I went towards. Now I am a motorcycle owner who wants to be a motorcycle rider but can't because his ride is in the shop.

Isn't life like that also? What you focus on is what you wind up in? If you focus on your problems, then your problems become the most important thing in your life. But, if you will focus on the Creator and King who gives you life, you will see past the problems and He will become the Center of your life.

What are you focusing on today? If you will look past your problems and focus on God, He will help you with your problems and they will take their proper place as a situation to be dealt with and not a mountain that is insurmountable. Look to God. Let Him keep you out of the ditch. Change your focus. Don't look at your problems. Look through them to the One Who can and will help you roll on past them.

IF THERE WAS EVER A QUESTION ABOUT LOVE, IT'S ANSWERED

"Greater love has no one than this, that one lay down his life for his friends."
John 15:13 (New American Standard Bible)

In the Spring of 2010 I had a serious health issue, a triple by-pass operation. Elain and I read, researched, confabbed with experts, did everything we thought we needed to do to get ready for this, but guess what? We weren't.

What was supposed to be just a five day stay at most turned in to twenty-three days and nights. They tell me I nearly died on three different occasions. I don't know. I kind of slept through most of it. My kidneys failed. My lungs failed. I got pneumonia, a staph infection and a bacterial infection just for good measure. A great time was had by all!

Through all of this, Elain, my bride, stayed with me through each one of those twenty-three days and nights in the hospital. I ate tasteless food. She ate tasteless food. I slept (if you want to call what I did sleep) and so did she only not as much as I did and on a very small couch. I dealt with "not too professional" health workers. She actually dealt with them more. I found out that a hospital is not a good place to be sick. And I also found out if you're going to be in the hospital more than overnight, you better have an outspoken advocate with you. She was there for me in ways that I never dreamed of.

Elain, my precious bride of thirty three years stood with me and stayed with me. She bathed me, cleaned me, fed me, cleaned up after me. She did things for me that, had I been cloned, I wouldn't have done for me. The entire time without a word of complaint to me, and with such an attitude of care, love and servanthood that I was truly blessed to be in her presence.

When we finally left the hospital and got home, there would be more of the same. I was a physical wreck for quite a while before I started turning the corner on getting healthy again. The heart wasn't the problem, everything else was. I had more tubes and things that made strange noises stuck in me and dangling from me, Frankenstein's monster would have said, "gross".

Well, you read above how long Elain and I have been married and the entire time there has never been a question of her love and devotion to me in my mind. However, after this event, incident, trauma and drama, I have seen her show a greater love and devotion for me than I could imagine. She nursed me back to health with as much attitude as action. No matter what happens the rest of our lives, I will never question her love for me just because of what she went through with my illness. She actually proved something that didn't need proving. Why? Not because she felt she needed to prove it, but because she already loved me that much. This happening was just the task in front of her. She did it because that was part of being married to and in love with me. No bands, no banners, no medals, just "I love you" and today this is what I need to do for you.

There is One in all of our lives Who set Himself aside to be a servant for us all. He set aside royalty in Heaven. Know anyone else that would do that for you, I don't. Then He came to Earth taught us, showed us how to live and then died for us, a horrible death because that was the task in front of Him. No bands, no banners, no medals, but rather this was how He showed His love for us, doing what needed to be done.

I pray that you have someone in your lives like I have Elain in mine. Are you in someone's life that way? That kind of love has now been shown to me in multiple ways, I read about Jesus doing that for me in the Bible and, quite honestly, I did understand it with my mind. However, I've now seen Elain do it first hind and I understand it with my heart. This is truly great love.

INK PINK, DO YOU STINK?

"For as he thinketh in his heart, so is he. . ."
Proverbs 23:7 (King James Version)

We know someone who smokes. When we go to their house although they may not even smoke while we're there, we still smell like smoke when we leave. They don't get it. They believe that since they aren't smoking in front of us, it shouldn't matter. However, we must put whatever we were wearing in the wash to get the smell out of it. What also has happened is that they don't even realize that there is a smell because it has so permeated everything in their lives. Taste, smell, both are effected by the cigarette smoke.

Sin is like that also. I'm not here to preach against smoking, just read the side of the cigarette package. If a product is so bad for you that a warning that 'this stuff can kill you' is on the side, that should be enough. I'm here to tell you that the life that you are living is leaving a "smell" on you that others can smell. The question is, "what do you smell like?" Are you giving off a odor that would have the dog run under the house, or a scent that the perfumers of Paris would be envious of?

Here's the bottom line of what I'm trying to tell you, sin lingers. We may think that what we do goes away as soon as we stop for the moment, but it doesn't. The places you go, the things you do, the people you run with, go with you. You may not think so, but they do. Your attitude and your actions are affected by where you go, what you do, and whom you do it with. And when you are around those who you don't really want to know about your "other life", quite often they are aware. I can't tell you how many times I've had people talk to me and try to pretend that they aren't living that "other life", but I know they are. There's an old saying, "if you lie down with dogs, you'll get up with fleas". And as we all know, it's no fun to be around a flea bitten hound. Remember, I live with four hounds and it is very easy to have a flea invasion at anytime.

Here's another question. "Is any of the garbage part of you life really helping you"? Is it really making you happier or more of a joy to be around? Are you really more popular because you can out drink, out curse, out gossip, out whatever others? Or does it just make you feel that way for a short time and when you are alone at 3 A.M., or looking at yourself in the mirror the next morning are you embarrassed?

Then why do it? There is a person and there is a place where you can put that old life, that old person behind you. The person who loves you is Jesus Christ. The place where people care is the church. I know some churches treat the ones who are most in need like they're not wanted, and for that please accept my apology. But there are those places where you will find love, fellowship, direction and the more complete life you have been searching for. Find that place. Don't quit looking, don't give up until you do. You are worth it. If God hasn't given up on you, and He hasn't, I can tell that because you're still alive. Don't give up on yourself.

JUST POINT AND CLICK, ITS THAT SIMPLE

"For by grace you have been saved through faith; and that not of yourselves, it is the gift of God;"

Ephesians 2:8 (New American Standard Bible)

The other day I was writing a sermon on my computer. I was sitting there, thinking deep theological thoughts as I do, such as, "why do my eyes feel straight, but my glasses are crooked?" Or "How much is enough milk on my cereal?' You know those thoughts, you have them sometimes. As I went to close the document which is just a fancy way of referring to the stuff I had written, I really looked at something I had seen hundreds of times before. I could point and click at a certain place on my computer and everything I had done would be "saved." What a wonderful thought, point, click, BOOM, saved. For eternity all of my thoughts and writings would be kept, never to diminish or corrupt. They were protected and sealed just by performing a simple task called saving. You know where I'm going don't you?

It's just about that simple for us. God has done the work. God has made the provision-- the way for us to be saved. All we have to do is point ourselves to Him. Ask Him to save us, and BOOM, just that quickly we are sealed forever by Him and His perfect graceful act in our lives.

Today in your life, does it feel like the next power surge will knock you "off line?" Is everything you've done in life going to save you, or would it all be lost forever just because you didn't feel it necessary to be "saved" today?

Well, it's clouding up outside now. I think I'll be safe and go ahead and save what I have written thus far. Isn't your life important enough that it, that you should be saved? How about your spouse? Your children? Your other loved ones? Shouldn't that be taken care of today, right now? If you don't know what to do, just ask God, He will find you someone who will help. You think that computer has a lot of answers, imagine all the answers the Creator of the universe has for you and wants to give to you, along with more love than you can ever imagine. Try to get that from your computer. "Saved". That has a good sound to it, doesn't it?

THE DAY I BECAME, "THE HEADACHE"

"He that dwelleth in the secret place of the most High shall abide under the shadow of the Almighty."
Psalm 91:1

Throughout my life there have been many times I have been referred to as a headache. Churches, denomination, my bride, even as hard as this may seem to believe, teenage daughter—all have felt that I was a pain at some time or another. But never, never have I been referred to as THE headache. That all changed a few years back. Forgive me for having to give you a history of the world story in order to make a point, but I want to make sure that you get everything I want you to get out of this. Also you may find that there isn't as much humor in this story as in some. For me, when the grim reaper may be holding my number, quipping goes down, "help me Father" goes up.

On a Sunday morning I got a headache. No big deal. I live in south Louisiana and sinus headaches are something you get when you live in a high humidity climate. The problem was this, by Monday I thought someone was dancing on my head in football shoes. Matter of fact, I thought a football team was dancing on my head in football shoes. Tuesday I went to the doctor and was diagnosed with a migraine headache. No history of them in my family, but you have to start somewhere. The doctor gave me medicine that didn't make a dent in the headache and the next day moved on to "heavier" meds. Thursday evening I felt slightly better. So far for the week, everything I had eaten had revisited me by means of the same path, I thought that maybe now, I could eat something. At 3:30 A.M. on Friday it all started over again worse that ever before. A few hours later I was in the emergency room of a hospital dealing with something totally foreign to my thought processes, being really sick.

As Elain and I spent our time in the ER we talked, gave our thoughts as to what was happening here and wished that the doctors would hurry up, give me a shot for whatever this was. During this time, I became "the headache". As they started to run tests, nurses and others would come into the room, ask if this was "the headache" and take me elsewhere to do that magic they do.

I don't know if you have ever heard or seen things in your life that your mind would not accept what your eyes had seen or perhaps your ears had heard. I had that happen that morning. A very kind rather ashen faced doctor came into my room and said, "I have some disturbing news." Now I don't know your definition of "disturbing", let me give you mine: the restaurant is closed, no refunds for any reason, what's that on the floor, (this would be a Biscuit and Catfish thing), but never what the doctor was about to say. "You have a blood clot on your brain." Do you want a D word for that kind of news? How about devastating, demoralizing, destroyed or distraught. Any or all of the above, but not just "disturbing". After the initial shock, the doctor told us that the best neuro surgeon in town was on duty at another hospital near by and that she would like to send me to him.

The next thing I know, I am flying down the hall sometimes forward, sometimes backward, sometimes side ways on my way to an ambulance for the next part of my "disturbing" journey. Please understand my warped sense of humor. As I lay in the ambulance on the ride, I'm still trying to make jokes and "keep it light" with the emergency technicians. Maybe I thought that if I didn't treat this too seriously then it wouldn't be. (I know, warped thinking).

While making the trip to the second hospital, the EMT's had questions to ask concerning my situation. "Have you received a blow to the head? This is quite often caused by a blow to the head." I responded with what I thought was quite cute, "Elain hits me in the head during the night". They laughed, got quiet for about 10 seconds and then asked, "sir, does she really?" I soooo had her in my hands right then. What could she do to me? I was sick. Actually she could do a lot so I quickly let that joke go.

The ride in the ambulance wasn't fun. No lights. Nor siren. Just lay there. No one to wave to and even if I did, they wouldn't see me. Years of our daughter Ari being in parades were being wasted, I KNEW HOW TO DO A PARADE WAVE. Wrist, wrist. Elbow, elbow. Touch the pearls. Change hands. Wrist, wrist. Elbow, elbow. Touch the pearls. But we'll get back to the ambulance ride later. I did some learning there. That's where philosophy and reality met.

Intensive Care Unit. This is not a place to rest. It is a good place to be sick. Maybe even to get well, but you won't rest there; too noisy; beeps; talking; people in and out; way too much commotion. This is the place where you are awaken in the middle of the night to give you medicine to help you rest. You ask for food and they put some liquid in you. I remember being hungry, asking for food and being told that I couldn't have any. "why? I asked. "Because you threw up" I was told. "I've thrown up before and always been able to get back on that horse" I responded. Once again, I became "the headache". However now I was "the blood clot in room 6. One of the things that gets me about this is that I am a rather intelligent individual. I have command of the English language and graduated from a very fine seminary. All of a sudden to these people I became a 2 year old nincompoop with milk and corn flakes dripping from my chin and no idea of how to think or respond to questions. As a matter of fact, about the only thing good about ICU was the fact that as the pain in my head would really get to me, I could get more morphine like you get a refill on your soft drink at McDonald's. It really stuck in my mind here, to these two doctors in the room with me , mere feet from my head and with a chart in their hands that had my name in it, I was the blood clot in room 6. To God, Who kept up with all of creation and everything since then, He still knew my name. The same as He knew the stars, He knew me. I was His child who was sick. If you ever think that you don't matter, if you don't think that anyone cares, remember no matter what, God knows who you are and cares enough about you to know your name, your circumstances and despite all in our lives, enough to die for us and carry our burden to His grave and our hopes to His Father. No matter what a headache you are or I am, we're His and He loves us.

I told you we would get back to something important during the ambulance ride and this is it. After the tests, conversations and "disturbing news" we received at the first hospital I was hoisted into an ambulance to go where the neuro-surgeon was. As the emts closed the doors to the back of the ambulance, quite honestly I wondered if I had heard Elain's voice for the last time. It's a scary place to be. As I road in the ambulance I began asking myself questions like this, "do you believe what you've been preaching?" The Scripture that kept coming to mind was "absent from the body, present with the Lord." Do you really believe this? You're facing death, do you believe?

The word sealed was what came to my mind. "You are permanently sealed". Now I don't know if you believe in receiving words from God, but I do. It's Scriptural. If you don't believe, that's ok. If you don't believe that two plus two equals four, that's also ok. But remember this, it doesn't make the math wrong, it makes you wrong. Back to sealed, I remember growing up with a mother who would preserve fruit and stuff in the summer for winter's use. The jars would be sealed to keep the contents from getting out or from bad stuff getting in. In the ambulance I realized that my life was sealed. My heart broke that I may never hear my bride or daughter's voice again. That I might not be at her wedding, never bounce grandchildren on my knee. That I would never see anyone I cared about again, but my life was sealed. If these were my last moments on earth, my loving Father was prepared to take me into a place of eternal bliss in His presence forever more in the next moment. Three things were laid to rest and sealed in the back of that ambulance: my hope, my faith and my commitment to Him. According to the writer of Hebrews, Chapter 11, verse 1 to be exact, he states, "What is faith? It is the confident assurance that what we hope for is going to happen. It is the evidence of things we cannot yet see."

For those who don't have a good working definition of hope, it is confident expectation. Not some wishful thinking, three coins in a fountain stuff, but rather something to hold on to when times are hard, the concrete realization that things will get better. I knew that no matter what happened in that ambulance, I would get better. If it meant in the hospital or in heaven, I would get better. Which brings to mind another verse from Hebrews found in Chapter 11, verse 6, "So, you see, it is impossible to please God without faith. Anyone who wants to come to him must believe that there is a God and that he rewards those who sincerely seek him. And that my righteousness must exceed that of the Pharisees..."

How can this happen? How can I know more, do more, be more closely joined with the righteousness they learned, inherited, lived with and taught? Simple, my righteousness comes from Jesus not from self. If you ever think you've arrived, it proves you haven't. My faith was sealed by the righteousness that Jesus imparted to me and therefore He sealed me as His own. Jesus Himself said, "For I tell you that unless your righteousness surpasses that of the Pharisees and the teachers of the law, you will certainly not enter the kingdom of heaven." Matthew 5:20

What is faith? It is our hand reaching out to His and saying, "you are Who You say You are." We must recognize Him for Who He is in order to please Him. No doing, no giving, no singing, no churching can replace that. Finally, my commitment to Him was sealed. If you're not dwelling in the shadow of the Most High on dear old earth, you won't in the life to come. You might want to read all of Psalm 91. Is your life sealed like that? If not, why not? It can be today.

THE PIERCING IS THE HARD PART

> "...for all have sinned and fall short of the glory of God."
> Romans 3:23 (New American Standard Bible)

I am a diabetic. Thanks for your prayers, however it is kept under control by diet and medication. But being a diabetic, I check my blood sugar levels on a regular basis. I "pop" myself with a piercing object that has a sharp needle in it, (wouldn't you hate it if it was a dull needle?). I cock the thing like you would a gun, put it on the tip of a finger and impale my myself for my long range health. Many have told me, "you must be used to it by now". Wrong. You never get used to sticking a sharp object in your finger. It's like living in the deep South, people elsewhere in the world tell me that "I must be used to the heat by now." I'm just as used to it as sticking my hand in a hot oven every day. You don't get used to it, you just learn to tolerate it. But as usual, I digress, back to the diabetes.

I saw a commercial on television the other day with the great blues singer and guitarist, B. B. King. He also is a diabetic. He was there as a salesman for a new glucometer that reads your blood sugar count using less blood. Here's how the process works: with the new monitors you can use less blood, therefore you can stick yourself other places than just your finger tips. Arm, leg, someone else, (just joking), but you get the picture. After that, you place the now less blood than before on a small rectangular strip that has been stuck in the end of the monitor and it tells you by number what your "blood count" is. Then you know if you're high or low and how to deal with it. My thought when I saw this was simple. "B. B., it's not the amount of the blood, it's sticking myself that hurts". It doesn't matter if it's one drop or two, needle, stick, pain, got it? And yet, if we don't stick ourselves, nothing happens. The piercing is necessary, but it's the hard part.

We look at Jesus the same way too many times. "I'm not as bad as him. That guy in jail, that abusive mother, that crack head. So what?" " All have sinned and fallen short of the glory of God". Do you know what that means? I'm glad you asked. It means that Jesus had to be pierced for you and for me every bit as much as He did for the worst sinner on the planet. Jesus had to be pierced just as much for me as He did for Adolph Hitler, Saddam Hussien, or Osama bin Laden. I remember being in an apartment one time and explaining the concept of "all have sinned and fallen short of the glory of God". We were on the top floor. I told the person I was explaining to that if we tried to jump to the next building, it wouldn't matter if we fell short by 5 feet or 5 inches, next stop concrete below. It's the same thought. We all fall short. Whether its's 5 feet or 5 inches, we all fall short. Therefore, Jesus had to be just as pierced for the person who falls short by 1 inch, the same as He does for the person who falls short by 1 mile. It's not the amount of blood that He had to shed for us, for me, it's the piercing. He had to die just as much for my sins as He did for anyone's.

Whenever you "get on your high horse", as we say in the South, remember, it's not the amount of the blood and it's not the amount of sin, it's the piercing that's the necessary part, but it's the hard part as well.

---------------- ----------------

WALKING, SWIMMING, OR RIDING A BICYCLE

"WHOEVER WILL CALL ON THE NAME OF
THE LORD WILL BE SAVED."

Romans 10:13 (New American Standard Bible)

I had high cholesterol. It's a problem that really doesn't manifest itself in any outward way until the stroke or the heart attack happens. It just stays there, sneaks up on you and then kills you or at least cripples you in one form or another.

I met with my one of my doctors about this, not "Dr. Here's-Another-Pill", but my other doctor who was willing to talk about what I could do to make it better. Most of the time we want doctors to take the responsibility to "fix" us and we don't want to take responsibility for any part of what needs to be done. This doctor told me that I had a part to play in this. "IF" I wanted to get better, "I MUST"... Don't you hate that word, "IF", just fix me and let me get on my way. That's what we want.

Anyway, the doctor said that I must spend 30 minutes a day, 5 days a week doing aerobic exercise in order to keep my heart in shape and strengthen it. She said that this exercise could be done by walking, swimming, or riding a bicycle. MY TURN! I went into my "sales pitch" for what I wanted to do and how I wanted to do it. I told her how I lifted weights and did other similar exercises which would do the same thing. She patiently sat there, let me finish and repeated, "walking, swimming, or riding a bicycle", were the ONLY exercises that would accomplish what needed accomplishing in the case of high cholesterol. I tried to appeal to her sense of "fair play" and compromise with this for that and that for this. "Walking, swimming or riding a bicycle" was once again the directions I was given, IF I wanted to yada, yada, yada...

It finally dawned on me that her health would not be affected either way if I did, or didn't do what she was telling me to do. It was all for me. If I wanted to get better, I'd better do what she says. I'm the one who would have the stroke or the heart attack. Everything she said was for my benefit.

We most certainly do this with God. He has told us how to get to Him. How to become one of His children, a part of His kingdom. Simply put--Jesus Christ. Jesus stated in John 14:6, "I am the way and the truth and the life. No one comes to the Father except through Me." Yeah, but what about my hard work. "You want to get to the Father, its through Me." How about the money I gave to the charity? "You want to get to the Father, its through Me." Let's face it folks, some of us think we should be allowed in Heaven just because we eat all our vegetables and don't litter. God is very specific. "If you want to get to Me, you'll do it through my Son." PERIOD.

Let's quit dancing around the issue. Quit trying to make God meet us on our terms. He has laid out how we can get to Him and it's not for Him, it's for us. He will still be God no matter what we do. He sent His Son for me and IF I want my life to be better, I MUST do it His way. Quit playing. It's not walking swimming, or riding a bicycle. He's done the work. He's done the dying. All we have to do is accept what He's done for us by reaching out our hand of faith to Him and WE WILL BE SAVED. Not kind of saved. Not "fixing to be saved." But totally, completely, and permanently saved. Don't waste time. The enemy is sitting out there waiting for that time to kill, steal, or destroy our lives, our homes, our marriages and our families. WHAT ARE YOU WAITING FOR?

WHEN BOUNCING OFF OF THE EDGE, YOU NEED YOUR FATHER'S ARMS

"Put on the full armor of God, so that you will be able to stand firm against the schemes of the devil. For our struggle is not against flesh and blood, but against the rulers, against the powers, against the world forces of this darkness, against the spiritual forces of wickedness in the heavenly places. Therefore, take up the full armor of God, so that you will be able to resist in the evil day, and having done everything, to stand firm."

Ephesians 6:11-13 (New American Standard Bible)

I can remember as a small boy, once or twice during the Summer, my family would make a daytrip from our home in Monroe to a place called Volman's Lake. I was so young then that I don't even know if that is the right spelling. It was such a special event, being one of five children and my father being a letter carrier for the Post Office, well special events were just that, special. I can remember the anticipation I felt as we got closer and the question of, "how much farther," had just about worn out it's welcome on my parents ears and nerves.

I can see in my mind as I ran from the car, despite impassioned pleas and threats concerning safety, across sand, mud, rocks and dirt to make it to the water's edge. We weren't allowed to go in without my father, mom was a land-lubber, and he would have to take his time unloading the car of the picnic delicacies which we would be able to feast on as the day progressed. The morning of romping in the surf, ok there was no surf but at age 6 you take what you can get, was only equaled by the blanket full of food that was waiting us at lunch time.

After lunch and the proper time element, I think it was 30 minutes or 30 days they both seemed very long at that age, I was allowed to go back into the water. This time however, I didn't wait on my dad, I went on ahead without him. As I stood in the water about chest high with my back to the lake and my eyes towards the bank I would bounce up and down having the time of my life. Everything was fine until I accidentally bounced backward too far and slipped off into a deeper part of the lake. Now my bouncing took on a whole new meaning. Since I couldn't swim, I now had to bounce to keep the water from going over my mouth and face and cutting off my air supply. Panic set in. What had been fun, that I was in control of, or so I thought, was now a situation that threatened my life.

Out of nowhere I glimpsed my father as his arms swooped down and pulled me out of the grip of something that threatened my very existence. I hadn't had time to call out, wave my arms nor did I really even see him. Fortunately, he was watching me and when he saw me going under, he came to my rescue.

Isn't that how we treat sin in our lives? We think that we can "dabble" in it, pick it up, put it down whenever we like? We think that we can control it and don't realize that we can't until it's "over our heads".

Fortunately, we also have a Father that watches out for us better than we watch out for ourselves. He's there with arms that want to swoop down and help us when we "go off of the deep end".

If right now you're "bouncing as high as you can", yet the world and all of its temptations are still getting the better of you, just hold up your arms and open your heart, to your Father in Heaven. He wants to save you, to hold you and to keep from drowning in a sea that's too big for us. He longs to be your Protector and your Provider. Won't you let Him?

ONLY 30 MINUTES IS 30 MINUTES

"Be diligent to present yourself approved to God as a workman who does not need to be ashamed, accurately handling the word of truth."

2 Timothy 2:15 (New American Standard Bible)

I work out. You know, exercise. Not as often as I should nor as extensively as I should, but I work out. I have some weights at home along with a treadmill. I do about 30 minutes on the treadmill as often as I can which translates into about one and one half to one and three quarters miles. (Shut -up, that's a good work out for me). The key is thirty minutes on the treadmill. My doctor told me that I need to get my heart rate up to about 80% of capacity for thirty minutes for a good cardiovascular work out.

As I have done this I have found that I can go faster on the treadmill or, weather permitting, when Elain and I can do the same thing outside, but no matter how fast we go, uphill or down, the key is 30 minutes. You can't do a thirty minute walk faster than thirty minutes. Logical? As we have done this for years it has gotten to be a time when we can talk about the cares of the day or just be together. But a thirty minute walk has to be a thirty minute walk.

Where am I going with this nonsense? No, I'm not trying to sell you my diet book, although you would like it, it includes ice cream. What I'm trying to say is that with the really good things in life there are no short cuts. Thirty minutes of walking can only be accomplished by walking thirty minutes. Time with family can only be accomplished by time with family. Time with God. A deeper relationship with God can only be accomplished by having a deeper relationship with God. Not more money. Not a bigger Bible. Time.

The more I work out, the more I want to work out. It is not a chore any more, it is something I enjoy. As I have matured in my faith, the more time I spend with my Heavenly Father the more I get out of the relationship. Scripture passages come alive. I receive more direction, more encouragement from the words written. I can hear and understand His voice more clearly. But what has it taken? Time. I know what you're going to say, " I don't have time for that". Well what is it that you do have time for? You have the same number of hours in the day as everyone else. Know this, you make time for what's important. I know that. You know that. If television is more important, then that's what you'll make time for. These days TV is truly what it use to be referred to as when it was called the vast wasteland but that's not what we're here to talk about.

The bottom line about our relationship with our Father is this, first we can never put in what He's put in. He has put the life of His one and only Son on the Cross for us. But we need to know this, if we don't put anything into our relationship with Him, we'll get nothing out of our relationship with Him. If you met someone that you fell head over heals in love with, would you spend time with them or would you just want to sing a song or two and think about them only twice a year, let's say, Christmas and Easter? Of course not. You would want to spend all the time you could with that person and when not with that person you would be thinking about and telling others about him or her. Right? If you truly loved that person you would put everything you have into your relationship including yourself. You would want to spend every minute you could with them.

You can spend time with God just about anywhere, home, car, office. Just take a minute and do it. The Bible tells us to pray without ceasing. You know how I do that? I never say Amen. When something or someone comes to mind, I pray right then. Let me suggest that when driving you don't close your eyes and bow your head but you know what I mean. I have a saying, aren't you surprised, "if it's important enough to pray about, it's important enough to pray about now".

Give yourself over. He gave all for you. He died for you. He doesn't want you to die for Him. He wants you to live for Him. A full abundant life. John 10:10. But you get out what you put in. If you put nothing into a relationship, you will get nothing out of that relationship. The price has been paid. All our Father asks of you is to take it, to reach out your hand of faith and take eternal life with Him that He had always had for us but we blew it. What's holding you back? Shame? Don't let it. There's nothing in your life bigger that God's forgiveness. It's there waiting. He's there waiting. Put yourself into the relationship, you'll get a new you out of it. But remember, only 30 minutes is 30 minutes, there are no short cuts.

SOMETHING FOR NOTHING? IT AINT SO.

"For the wages of sin is death, but the free gift of God is eternal life in Christ Jesus our Lord."

Romans 6:23 (New American Standard Bible)

Everything costs. There's no free ride. No free lunch. No free shoes, unless of course they're "hand me downs". There is a price to be paid for everything that is, was and ever will be. Oh yeah dude, butterflies are free. No they aren't. The next time you are at Ye Olde Butterfly Shoppe, just try and walk out without paying for that bucket of butterflies. Air is free. Wrong again. In places all over the world, making air breathable is extremely expensive. Nothing is totally free. It, whatever it is, has cost someone something. Great or small, something.

I enjoy watching commercials on television with offers that are beyond belief. You know the ones I'm talking about. You can buy the whatever product for $19.95 and get $9000 worth of additional stuff for free. Oh and by the way, the $19.95 thing is usually an $80 value. This line of thinking brings up many questions. You know, things that make you say hmmmm. First off, think of this. Usually these things are things that are "not sold in stores". Then what makes these people think that they are an $80 value. If they've never been sold any place and no one has ever paid $80 for them, then how are they an $80 value? Secondly, the extra stuff. How can they give that to me for free? Answer. They can't. No one can stay in business giving stuff away. Then all I have is a charge for shipping and handling. What's that about? Since this stuff is "not sold in any store", how else was I going to get it if they didn't ship it to me? Was I going to drop by their warehouse in lower Slobovia and pick it up? And what is handling? Was this miracle product going to ever get to me unless somebody put it in a bag, or a box or a something? These people didn't know that there was going to be a cost to get the whatever from point A, them, to point B, me?

Then what do they do? They tell me that if I will call in to them in the next 10 minutes they will double my order. Next thing that happens? A digital clock pops up on the screen and begins the descent from 10 minutes to zero which is when the offer expires and the world ends, or we get back to the movie on television, whichever comes first. Now we have a million dollar answer to all of my problems for only $19.95, plus shipping and handling. I'm staring at the tv, totally mesmerized by the opportunity I have been blessed with, not even trying to figure out what I would actually do with a hair dryer stand, hydraulic paint brush, moo moo maker, diet pills that will make me lose 200 pounds on an all ice cream diet or a laser light level which actually goes around corners. OK. That last one I really want. Don't know what to do with it, but I'm still yelling at Elain that I NEED one of those. Bottom line? If it sounds too good to be true, it usually is. Except one.

Approximately 2000 years ago a price was paid for something that you and I desperately needed, could not possibly afford and was purchased by One who didn't owe it and didn't need it. What was it? Salvation. Rightness with God. Who paid it? Jesus. But you knew that, didn't you? It was a very simple transaction. "The wages of sin is death". Now notice that I said simple, not easy. There was no bargaining, no haggling, no negotiating, that was the price. Death. Someone had to die. Herein lies the problem. It had to be Someone who had the right worth for the transaction. Someone perfect. Quite simply, you nor I have the right coinage, the right Visa or Master Card to pay for this. No matter how we try, this still couldn't be done in "three easy payments of whatever". It was one payment, right then, for everyone for all time and was paid for at the Cross. How much did Jesus pay? Everything. All He had. He had already set aside His royalty in Heaven to come to Earth to show us the way. There was a cost there. Now He had to pay with His life for a debt He didn't owe. Does this sound unfair to you? It does to me. But in this case, thank You Father for unfair. Many people say that they want God to be just. If He were just, what I just described would have never happened. Be careful what you ask for.

Now our part. All I had to do, all you have to do, is believe that what has been told you about Jesus in the Bible is true. That He truly is Lord. That He truly did come to Earth to show us the way. That He truly did die for my sins and yours. Again, quite simple. Remember that clock that I was talking about earlier? There is one ticking here. We have no idea when the time will expire. When the time does expire, it will be too late to take advantage of this offer. I've seen people make it. I've seen people miss it and I'll tell you this. No one that made it has ever regretted taking advantage of the greatest offer imaginable. Purchased by Jesus and given freely to us as a gift from God. Don't let <u>this</u> offer pass you by.